What I Learned about Leadership from My Dog

By John Covington

"What I Learned about Leadership from My Dog," by John Covington. ISBN 978-1-62137-110-6 (Softcover); 978-1-62137-129-8 (Hardcover); 978-1-62137-111-3 (eBook).

Published 2012 by Virtualbookworm.com Publishing Inc., P.O. Box 9949, College Station, TX 77842, US. ©2012, John Covington. All rights reserved. No part of this publication may be reproduced, stored in a retrieval system, or transmitted in any form or by any means, electronic, mechanical, recording or otherwise, without the prior written permission of John Covington.

Manufactured in the United States of America.

Endorsements

"John understands dogs, people, and organizations. With great wit he intertwines leadership theory, his experience in business and dog training. An entertaining and educational read."

Dr. Phillip Westbrook
Director of the Blackburn Institute, University of Alabama

"John has done it again! Making the jump from his first book, *Let's Don't Pave the Cow Paths* to his most recent book, *What I Learned About Leadership from My Dog,* is like getting a strong dose of leadership common sense from a fire hose. These two relatively short books are chucked full of folksy stories of John's personal leadership experiences with employees, peers and managers in his long career as a chemical engineer, consultant and perhaps most important, as a dog owner, lover and trainer. Getting to know John and his folks at CCI has certainly helped prepare me for my retirement as I face the seemingly never ending challenge of demonstrating to my wife Carol and our six year old Havanese pup Bentley as to which one of us is really the leader of the pack at our house".

Tom Patterson
Chairman of the Board
DAXKO, Inc

"John's refreshing book brings together insights from the two worlds of leadership theory and practice and of interaction with dogs. The intersection of these worlds invites and surprises with new ways to consider a leader's roles and functions. Read this book to find a different window through which to see the work and responsibilities of a leader."

Rev. Karen Greenwaldt
Chief Executive Officer
General Board of Discipleship
The United Methodist Church

"John managed to set a cadence to the narrative of his new book. Each new chapter and fresh idea is like the very beginning of a fireworks display. It opens up and sheds a different light on the topic. But then, the grand finale, it just goes pop, pop, pop, one nugget after another almost taking the breath away with so much wisdom. I see so many applications in our interactions with not only coworkers but family and friends alike."

Richard Legare
Mortgage Broker and Dog Trainer

"John's newest book lays out a compelling narrative on the essential elements of effective leadership on the training field and in the business field. His work is a reflection of his devotion to his dog Maggie and his business Chesapeake Consulting, Inc. In 1923, Max Emil Friedrich von Stephanitz, the founder of the modern-day German Shepherd Dog, wrote, "Show me your dog and I'll tell you what manner of man you are." Having watched John and Maggie work and train together these last few years, I can tell you that John is a gentle, compassionate, and devoted man. He has developed a relationship with Maggie that is truly build upon the foundations of trust and respect; the same elements that have created an outstanding leader in the business community. I thank John for sharing his passion and life lessons."

Charles Radle Jr.
Co-owner of Fieldstone Animal Inn and Dog Trainer

Acknowledgements

I am very thankful for all those that reviewed this book and gave me feedback including Dr. Karen Baldwin, Dr. Norm Baldwin, Leigh Covington, Linda Covington, Janet Dooley, Pastor Jim Farmer, Angelia Knight, Pastor Martha Meredith, Dr. Heath Turner and all of those who wrote endorsements.

A special thanks goes to Sean Wise, who provided the photographs.

I would also like to honor all those dogs that have taught me over the years especially Henry, Griffin, April, Heidi and, of course, our current dog, Maggie.

Table of Contents

Foreword 1

Preface 3

Chapter One:
Trust Your Dog and Consider Trusting Your People 7

Chapter Two:
Dogs and People — How Are They Alike? What Do
They Want? 14

Chapter Three:
House Breaking Your Puppies and Your Employees 24

Chapter Four:
How to Select Dogs and People; Is It the Same? 29

Chapter Five:
The Power of Focus – Get Better Results 38

Chapter Six:
In Order to Focus, We Must Learn to Trust 43

Chapter Seven:
Your State of Mind Affects Your Dog and Your People 48

Chapter Eight:
Rules and Obedience and How They Affect Creativity 53

Chapter Nine:
Reward, Punishment, and Stress 58

Chapter Ten:
Bias in Dogs and People; It's a Good and Bad Thing 64

Chapter Eleven:
Motivating Dogs and People 69

Chapter Twelve:
Training Dogs and People and How It Impacts Trust 74

Chapter Thirteen:
Communications and Listening with Dogs and Humans;
    Are We Listening? 82

Summary 85

Foreword

I grew up with a German Shepherd named Bullet ... like the one from the old Roy Rogers show. I just called him Bully because he weighed more than I did when we got him and he could wrestle me to the ground any time he chose to. I spent all of my teen years at home on a forty-acre plot of ground in northeast Alabama with Bully at my side most of the time. He saw us off to school, he welcomed us home, he went with me to feed the hogs, to milk the cow, to hunt squirrels, to fish, or just to roam. I learned that dogs are smart, or at least that Bully was smart...or maybe he was wise. He would not attack a snake while it was coiled regardless of what kind of snake it was. He waited until it started to crawl and then he was "on it". Bully was not a hunting dog per se, but he sure helped...most of the time. If it was squirrels we were hunting, he walked with enough noise that I could stand and wait for the squirrel to move around to my side of the tree. The squirrel thought he was hiding from a big dog, but he was really about to become breakfast. But Bully did get in the way hunting rabbits. You see, he was almost as fast as the rabbits, so he was usually too close for me to shoot. In fact if the rabbit ran in a straight line in the cotton field, Bully would catch him. He was one smart dog, mainly because he was good at listening to everything I needed to talk to someone about. And he would cock his head as if he understood.

The "trick" that always amazed me though, was how Bully could literally tackle me when I ran from him with a football. My brothers and I were always throwing a ball of some kind when we had free time. When one of us would catch the football and start running, Bully thought it was a personal challenge to him. He would grab the very bottom of our pant leg and throw his paw in front of us and trip us. It was great fun for all of us to play the game.

Bully was not well trained like the dogs you will meet in John's book, but he was good about the things for which I needed him to be good...hunting, sports, companionship, and listening. It was a relationship that I still feel good about. Would it not be good if we could feel good about all of our past relationships where we were the leader and someone else was our subordinate? Better still if those good memories are because of our effectiveness as a team. The real test of a good dog and master relationship is how they do as a team, each dependent on the other, each doing their job but not the job of the other (because they cannot). I think the analogy is that in a leader-subordinate relationship, it is because we should not try to do each other's job. And sometimes that is the first mistake of a leader.

I happen to believe that all of creation is well ordered and that we can learn lessons about some of the more complicated things from some of the more simple things. I am forever using analogies to communicate and to teach. When we see dogs and their master work, we sometimes think that it is simple. It is, to a real master trainer, but not to an amateur like most of us. Leadership is not simple, but it is easier to one who has mastered some of the principles involved. In this book "What I Learned about Leadership from My Dog", John Covington has focused on one leadership analogy and explored its many facets starting with trust and ending with communications. There are eleven other good facets in between those two. Study them as though they were facets on a diamond you are considering or actually buying. They just might be that valuable.

Tom Kilgore,
President and Chief Executive Officer
Tennessee Valley Authority

Preface

It has been my experience that we can learn a lot about life and important things by observing nature and things that might not be so obvious with regard to our leadership skills – such as dogs. God has created for us an earth full of education and learning experiences – all we need to do is stop, listen, and observe. When we get too close to issues involving our own leadership style, or even how others lead, we sometimes lose something; pride, ego, and territorial behavior may inhibit our senses. It is so easy to detach ourselves from the learning and to not do a proper self-examination. When dealing with your dog, it is difficult to run away from your leadership style. A famous saying among many a professional dog trainer is "Each handler gets the dog they deserve."

Is it the same way with our employees and our culture? Does each leader deserve the culture they have? If your dog's behavior is bad and you have owned the dog for a while, then my guess is you may have some personal leadership issues that you need to address. I certainly found some things in my personal leadership style that need addressing.

Experiences with handling both leadership positions and dogs have been a central part of my life since I was a child. I attended the United States Naval Academy where development of leaders is their stated mission and from there went on to gravitate to leadership positions in industry, church, and other non-profit organizations. I have owned and dealt with dogs all my life. I also have a deep passion for both topics.

The analogy of dog training and leadership of people is uniquely applicable and I think that connection will become more and more obvious as we go through this book together.

The topic of leadership is deep and it involves our personal relationships. If a topic mentioned in this book helps one person discover something that will help them in their own personal relationships, then the book is worth the effort to write. Can we humble ourselves and ask our dogs to teach us a thing or two about leadership?

Suzanne Clothier says in her book *If a Dog's Prayers were Answered Bones Would Rain from the Sky,* "To ask what can I learn from you is to open the door to an entire world of possibility in which our dogs can and do serve as our teachers." By learning practical techniques to maximize the utilization of the dog-human capability, we will also learn to do the same with the human-human capability.

Leadership is a personal and spiritual issue and one that carries with it enormous responsibility as to its impact on both people and dogs. The Monks of New Skete raise German Shepherds in their monastery in upstate New York. These monks put a holy dimension on working with dogs and feel that it is a mind-expanding experience. I certainly found this to be true. The subject matter of this book has taken me deeper than I expected and it has been fun.

In my last book on leadership, *Enterprise Fitness,* I outlined an overall leadership model that made sense to me and in the summary chapter I will outline how I think these two books weave together. However, I think this book is going to be more fun to write. We will talk about specific situations that we all address, and hopefully have a mind expanding experience by comparing the world of working with your dog to that of working with people.

Gaining a keener sense of self awareness is perhaps the single most important thing a leader can do. To understand how your behavior impacts others and your personal relationships with them is critical. We will find no better laboratory than our dogs.

Many dog training books focus on specific techniques to teach a variety of skills/commands; sit, down, come, stay, etc. There are a hundred ways to teach those commands and it is not as big of a deal as you might think. What is more important than the mechanics of training the technical skill for the dog, is training the human to be a better dog owner and to be a better leader. There needs to be a significant self-reflective aura to dog training, otherwise the potential for achievement between dog and handler is never approached.

Our company, Chesapeake Consulting Inc. (CCI), began focusing more on leadership when it became apparent to us that leadership drives culture and culture determined how successful a client would be implementing our process change technology. What we learned initially is that there are two basic models for leadership – an attribute model and a self-awareness model. In the attribute model, the attributes of a proven leader such as Churchill, Lincoln, Powell, etc. are defined and an individual leader is measured against those attributes. Then a gap analysis is done and the individual has an improvement plan based on that gap analysis. I think it is a laborious and stupid method – an individual spends their time trying to be someone else. In the self-awareness model, the leader learns how their own natural behavior may affect their relationships with others. This means not only understanding their own behavior, but having some insight into the behavior of those they lead so they can adapt their behavior to meet the other person at the best place. It does not imply being "false." In fact it is the opposite – it is simply being empathetic.

One of my good friends, Carol Ptak, recommended that I weave the evolution of CCI into the discussion. Carol is also an accomplished dog trainer and handler. I founded CCI in 1988 so I have raised her from a pup so using some examples in this book from over the last two decades will hopefully enhance our learning.

Many of the concepts such as "trust your dog" will appear in several chapters. This redundancy is done on purpose and is intended to enhance the chance that the reader will learn more from this book. I first learned about "spaced repetition" when I was deploying the DuPont STOP safety program in plants that I managed. The writers of the program claimed that retention on a concept could go from about 10% to over 80% by using the method. Maybe we even learned something new about leadership in the Preface? That would be cool.

There are seven things that I learned or re-enforced while writing this book:

1. Put more effort and science into the selection process.
2. Realize that we need to adapt our leadership style based on the person, situation, and time.
3. Leadership is about relationship and our level of self-awareness is a critical factor.
4. Trust your dog if you want better performance.
5. Be in the moment.
6. Learn the language of those you are leading.
7. Be more serious about dominion and its responsibilities.

Let's begin the journey with our canine friends.

Chapter One

Trust Your Dog and Consider Trusting Your People

It was a winter day in Patapsco State Park and Lucinda had gone off into the woods to hide and pretend like she was lost. Maggie, my female German Shepherd Dog (GSD) and I were to go find her. I was to supply the leadership and Maggie was to use her nose and sense of smell.

I have owned German Shepherds a good portion of my life and I just love the breed, although Maggie is the first dog I decided to put through a lot of formal training. Prior to Maggie I had always trained my dogs, and if I must say so, I did a good job. Novice dog folks would marvel at what April, Heidi (my other two GSD females), and Major could do. All my dogs had good "recall," which is dog people talk for "come." They could do a long stay and halt from a dead run which could have been a life-saving command if they were chasing a squirrel in front of an oncoming car.

My wife, Linda and I had gone about 20 years without a shepherd then we (I) got the itch. There was a breeder in Vance, Alabama (near Tuscaloosa) that had a litter of puppies and Linda called to see if I wanted one. I told her to get the largest female. We will learn later in the book that this is not the best way to select a puppy, but fortunately it has worked out great. I would not trade Maggie for a boatload of puppies.

Our trainer, Charlie Radle, said that the only thing you could get two dog trainers to agree on is how screwed up the third trainer is. I have found that to be true. Charlie had titled several shepherds in Schutzhund, which means "protection dog" in German. Schutzhund is a dog sport that has three elements to it: obedience, tracking and protection or, as some call it, "bite work." Bite work is where a dog runs and jumps on the person in the padded suit, it's not as bad as it sounds. For many dogs, bite work is an elevated game of tug of war.

One of the things that stuck with me was Charlie did less talking about training and more talking about establishing a relationship with your dog (does the same hold true for our employees?). He talked a lot about engaging in playing with the dog and that we were going to work on learning how to play. However, I am a tad impatient and sitting around learning how to play was going to test me. I now have a better understanding of what he was trying to convey. The fact is you can do both at the same time – train and play.

Maggie and I continued training on the elements of Schutzhund. She was excellent in obedience, ho-hum or worse in bite work, but loved tracking. In fact she is a tracking goddess. During this training I met Anne Wills, who is the founder of Dogs Finding Dogs, a search and rescue group for pets. I had checked into some traditional S&R groups but I got mostly negative feedback – they trained all the time, spent a lot of their own money, and never got called out to do much because the authorities would rather use their own K9 units. Pets get lost all the time. The principles of tracking are the same and you get to do a lot more work. It is also rewarding whenever you can reunite someone with their lost pet. The major issue for me was being able to work my dog and if in the process I could help someone else, then that's a really cool thing.

Most of our weekly training is finding humans and that is why Lucinda got lost. This was a big day for us because we had a brand new trainer, Janet Dooley. Our group had just come off a very bad experience with the previous trainer. That trainer had a low regard for the dogs and our ability as handlers. Training sessions were tense and we were not advancing and making progress. The trust level between handlers and the trainer was non-existent. We were all anxious to prove to Janet that we were good S&R teams so the heat was on Maggie and me to find Lucinda. There was some pride and ego at stake.

Off Maggie and I go and she is on the scent. Dogs follow a scent pattern that is composed of discarded skin, crushed vegetation, and ruptured soil. Here is a short explanation...

When you mow your grass it has a strong and pleasant odor that we all can detect. When you step on a blade of grass the same thing happens, however you and I cannot smell it, but your dog can. When you disrupt a big pile of compost it is easy for us to detect the odor. The same thing happens when you walk on the ground, however you and I cannot detect the smell, but our dogs can. Each of us flake off skin all of the time and when we walk, it falls to the ground and creates an odor. Thank heavens we cannot detect that as it probably has the aroma of my smelly feet.

Scent is like fallen leaves – the wind blows it around so environmental conditions must be taken into consideration when tracking. The best weather for tracking is moist with little or no wind and the worst condition is low humidity and windy.

Maggie tracked Lucinda down a dirt trail in the woods. All of a sudden she seemed to lose the scent and she wandered off to the left and into the woods. She stared out into the forest and seemed disinterested. Did she not understand that Janet was evaluating us and that she was making us look bad? I could sense myself getting a tad angry with her. She then took a poop – talk about lack of concern! "Poor Lucinda is lost and all you can do is stare out into the woods and take a dump?" Janet stands coolly off to the side with her arms crossed not saying a word. She then said, "Why don't you take her over here and cast her." Casting is a method of taking the dog back to where they had the scent and moving them in circles so they can reconnect with the scent. That worked like a charm and Maggie was back on the trail. It was not long before we found the long lost Lucinda standing behind a tree with a hand full of doggie snacks and a ball as Maggie's reward for finding her.

After the track, Janet got us around to recap. She started off by saying, "I hate the term crittering." Crittering is the dog handler term used for explaining that the dog is out to lunch (looking for critters) when they should be working. I guess she felt that is what I was going to blame our snag on, and she wanted to block that excuse from the start. She went on, "When Maggie loses the scent, no one is more upset than Maggie. She wants to do a good job and she is stressed out when she loses the scent. When she offers alternate behaviors such as looking off into the woods, she is showing signs of stress. The absolute worst thing you can do is get angry and make the stress worse. Your job is to relieve the stress and help her." And then she said something that I will never forget which might just be the theme of this book; "Trust your dog."

Crap – I just had my rear end chewed out by some lady young enough to be my daughter. Things got better and after several hours of training, Maggie hopped in the back seat of the car and we started home. I was thinking about the whole track with Lucinda and how I had reacted to Maggie. I couldn't help but ask myself the question; "Do I ever treat people like that?" I don't think I liked the answer. Does my ego get in the way of my leadership? Yes it does – it is the same old ego that also helps strain relationships.

Charlie had it correct – it is about relationships with your dog. For the most part, especially for larger dogs, the relationship must also be based on you being the leader. Leadership is simply a form of relationship – a deep one where you have been given the power by the other person to influence them from time to time. This relationship will be based on respect – either respect from being afraid of you or respect from trusting you. We want to embrace trust.

So what is the answer and recipe for establishing such relationships? Are they all the same? Let's look at a several dog-people relationships.

Maggie and I were walking by our local school and I saw a man playing with his German Shepherd off leash. Up until now, the only shepherds I had seen off leash in our neighborhood were Maggie and the police officer's K-9 that lived down the street. There was something special about this dog – he just had an air of confidence and composure about him. I put Maggie on a down command and went over to talk with the man. He introduced me to his dog, Dollar, who was nine years old and a retired Navy SEAL. The man was not the dogs' service handler but was the adopted "dad." It was a unique relationship between dog and man and on this occasion I give most of the credit to the dog. After talking with the man it was obvious he had so much respect for the dog that he did not view the animal as something inferior to himself; Dollar certainly felt that level of trust. I later pondered what Dollar had seen and experienced during his service career. How could you not be in awe and trust this dog? What if we had that type of thought process of trust and respect about all of our dogs? Would it make a difference in how we related to them and thus our ability to influence them? How about with the people we lead and spend time with?

I wonder how much of Dollar's obvious air of self-confidence and good nature was a reflection of all of the positive vibes he got from people. Everyone who met Dollar was made aware of his background as a Navy SEAL so he immediately won their respect. Dollar felt the trust others had in him for good cause. Somewhere along the line a sailor trusted Dollar with his life.

Several years ago a young lady, who was attending the Naval Academy Ring Dance, was staying at our home. It was my responsibility to get her to the airport on time to catch her flight back to Birmingham. I messed up and let the time get away from me. We were all in a panic as we only had a short time for her to catch her flight. Mary Ann, the young lady, Leigh, my daughter, and I rushed off to the airport. As we were speeding towards the terminal, I was barking out instructions to Mary Ann and Leigh. I told Mary Ann to concentrate on getting checked in with her luggage and my daughter Leigh to go down and stop the plane;

this was long before 9/11 and airport security was at the gate. When I gave Leigh those instructions, I had absolute confidence that she would accomplish the task – I trusted her. She was about 12 years old at the time. Leigh flies through the terminal, to the gate, down the ramp, and onto the plane and announced to the pilot and flight attendants; "Stop this plane, you must wait for Mary Ann!" The flight attendant looked at her and said, "Young lady, how did you get on this plane?" They waited for Mary Ann and all was well. There was never any doubt in Leigh's mind that she would stop the plane – she felt the trust.

Prior to founding CCI, my career involved leading and managing employees, and I was weary of having to deal with people. I did not want any more employees and I was perfectly content on doing everything myself and focusing on helping my clients. After about a year, I found myself swamped with work and tasks that needed to be done – I was going to have to hire someone else or go crazy. I made a list of everything I was doing and then went back and circled the items that only I could do. The list of circled items was a lot shorter and manageable. I needed to hire someone to deal with the items that were not circled. Andrea Siple was my first hire and my initial instructions to her were, "Your first job is to take care of all of the grief associated with hiring you, then address these non-circled items." Andrea was great and played a large role in our initial success as a company. Trusting Andrea was a good thing to do for everyone and for our brand new company.

Like humans, dogs are different and unique. Linda noticed the bag of cat food had a Cairn terrier rear-end sticking out of it. My little buddy Griffin had gotten into the closet, pulled out the cat food, and was in the process of chowing down. From Linda's perspective, this was a massive rule infraction. She playfully swatted Griffin's rear end and fussed at him to get out of the cat food bag. Griffin came out of the bag furious – teeth glaring, lips curled, and snarling at Linda – he even charged her letting her know that he had no intention of abandoning the bag. Linda snatched his little 20 pounds or so off the ground, put the cat food bag back in the closet, and closed the door. The incident was essentially over. That was just Griffin – our little enforcer. The only ones he did not mess with were me and Henry, the older Cairn. Both Henry and Griffin have since made their journey over the Rainbow Bridge, however Linda and I still laugh about the incident on numerous occasions as we reflect on our memories of our pets. I then said to Linda; "That would not have been so funny if it were Maggie." An 80 pound German Shepherd dominating you is an entirely different story and quite a scary one. Under no circumstances would we have let that happen. Our relationships with all of our pets are different because they have different personalities and are in different situations. In many respects our leadership style is the same, however it needs to be adapted for each pet. The same is true for humans as they also vary in behavior style.

Here is what we should learn from this chapter. We want to improve leadership and leadership is about relationships. In order to improve relationships, we must improve our level of trust. Trust is unique to each relationship we have and is largely dependent on our individual mindsets. The good news is we have the ability and can control improvement in this area; we control our own mindset. We can choose to trust or we can choose not to trust in any given situation.

Trust is situational. I trust Maggie's ability to track. I do not trust her to guard the pot roast. The same is true for the people you lead – there are things that fall into their wheelhouse of skill and knowledge and there are things that don't. Part of your job is to sort those out and set your employees up to win.

Trust must work both ways as you must gain the trust of those you lead. Admiral Chester Nimitz said, "Leadership may be defined as that quality that inspires sufficient confidence in subordinates as to be willing to accept his views and carry out his commands."

Chapter Two

Dogs and People — How Are They Alike? What Do They Want?

What about people and dogs? Who are they and how is their relationship with us relevant to our leadership in non-dog related roles in our life?

The first place to start is exploring the difference between dogs and people. The more one explores the world of dogs, the more that dogs gain in status. Suzanne Clothier and the Monks of New Skete feel that dogs are spiritual beings, just like humans. I recently read a quote, "If anyone doubts that a dog has a soul they have never gazed into the eyes of a German Shepherd." Throughout this book, I am going to lean on the expertise of dog trainers ranging from the monks and Clothier to those that make their business selecting, training, and selling K9's to the military and police departments. Just like in leadership and management theory, we will get to see several different perspectives. If we are fortunate, we will bask in the overlap and walk away with some useful methods to improve our own leadership.

So what is the difference between dogs and man? My knee jerk answer based on my background was the issue of "free will." Man has free will and animals don't. Well, that answers that question – except that I was wrong. When I call my dog, she can choose to come or she can choose not to come. I can feel and hear some of my dog training pals cringing and screaming at me, "Once the dog knows the command they MUST OBEY you." Yes, however they make that choice. When someone disciplines a dog, the animal can choose to bite or not bite.

I even posed the question to Pastor Martha Meredith, one of our preachers. "Pastor, what is the difference between dogs and people? The answer is not free will." She took a deep breath, probably wondering where she had gone wrong in her education of me and sighed – "Why do you ask such questions? God made man in his image and that does not necessarily mean physical image."

Thank you Pastor Martha! I got it now – God revealed himself in Christ so the answer must be in the "fruits of the Spirit" which are love, joy, peace, patience, kindness, goodness, faithfulness, gentleness, and self-control. We exhibit those and dogs do not.

Well that obviously isn't the answer because my dog shows more of those characteristics than I do.

I discovered the answer to be dominion. Man has dominion over the earth. Whether or not that was a good idea or not is beside the point. It's the answer I was searching for -- man has the responsibility of caring for the earth and her creatures. It is obviously an assumed leadership role for us all. When I bounced this off my good friend Carol Patterson, she suggested that my dominion would be in deep poop if I ran into a pack of hungry wolves in the Alaskan wilderness. I reminded her that in the battle of wolves versus humans unfortunately it has been a slaughter.

Our dominion has Biblical roots; God says to Noah and his sons: "The fear and dread of you will fall on all beasts of the earth and on all the birds of the sky, on every creature that moves along the ground, and on all the fish in the sea; they are given into your hands." Genesis 9:2.

With dominion there comes awesome leadership responsibility, and to some extent, all humans have this responsibility. Perhaps God gave us dogs to hone our leadership skills and to help us connect to the rest of nature rather than a life filled with things. Leadership cannot be a craving for power or arbitrary domination. Instead we must recognize our responsibility to help both dogs and people achieve their potential. We must be servant leaders.

How do you treat your dog? One of the main problems plaguing dogs is loneliness. The good Monks of New Skete claim that 80% of the problem dogs they deal with do not sleep in the same room with their owners – they are lonely. Your dog looks to you for protection, food, shelter, vet care, but most of all your attention and an ongoing relationship. Your dog wants to be with you, even if you are asleep. That is part of their pack animal instinct.

One dog trainer I met kept his personal dogs crated. He and his wife had about eight dogs and all were kept in crates in their garage. I was at their house one day before a class and questioned the practice. He said there was nothing wrong with keeping the dogs in crates and he tried to justify it by saying that wolves live in small dens. He then went on to say that all of his dogs were for sale at all times. One of the dogs crated was a yellow lab. The dog looked at me through the crate door as if to say "help." The fellow may claim to be an animal lover but he can't prove it by me. Good common sense needs to kick in with respect to caring for our animals and our employees.

Dog training aside, dog crates are wonderful tools in training and raising your dog. However under no means should it be the permanent abode for your pet.

How well do you do with your employees? Do you provide a safe work environment free of danger and harassment? Do you create a culture where people can thrive and perform well? Are you providing good leadership – giving it your best?

Let's explore dominion with an industrial example. I did not enjoy working at Sherwin-Williams and I was the plant manager of what was at the time their largest paint manufacturing facility. At that time the company was run by Jack Breen, and the man was just ruthless. There was a culture of hostility and cutting the head count seemed to always be the top item on the agenda. Make no mistake, Breen was an effective CEO and he saved Sherwin-Williams from bankruptcy, but I am not so certain that he needed to do it in the manner he did. Part of the budget process was to cut operating expenses which translated into a number of heads that a plant manager would have to chop. There was a lady in shipping that had a disdain for management and she was not shy about letting you know it. Every attempt I made to try and be nice to her was always met with a terse response, normally in front of other employees. I did not like her. When I got my number from corporate on how many heads I had to chop, she immediately came to my mind. The day of termination came and I summoned her to my office. I told her in a very professional way that she was terminated. I will never forget the look in her face and her body language. All of the aggression and surliness was gone. Then she said, "I am a single mom. I need this job. What am I going to do?" She was sincere in asking me the question as if I could help her. It was really uncomfortable that she was asking the person that had just fired her – "what am I going to do?"

Did I let her go because I didn't like her? I had "dominion" over the plant site, did I abuse my power? Was I a poor steward and misuse my dominion as a leader? Did my ego influence my leadership? It was a long time ago, so I just do not know the answer to all those questions but I will never forget the encounter. I am glad that the encounter nags me. Overall I left the plant in much better condition than I found it, so on my watch, I did a good job with the dominion I was responsible for.

What we do at CCI is help people improve their dominion. Years ago we did a project for what was then Grove Manufacturing in Pennsylvania. The plant was in chaos and many workers and supervisors could not remember the last day they had off. There was a lot of stress. The management team brought in to make things better were our friends, so we got involved. We were part of an improvement effort that ended up getting a lot more products manufactured with little or no overtime. I recall one of the supervisors thanking me for the "calm" we helped install. Our folks at CCI understand that is part of what we do – our responsibility.

What is a dog? Lord knows there has been a ton written on this and I will simply state some of what I have learned from those that have spent a lifetime studying the topic. Genetically, a dog is a micro gnat from a wolf. Even those dogs that look like dust mops are genetically close to the wolf. Dogs are pack animals, however to end your understanding there would be a mistake because dogs are individuals. There are some differences between dogs and wolves. Wolves hunt in packs, and dogs hunt alone, even if they are running in a pack. The big difference is how they view humans. Wolves will do all in their power to distance themselves from humans whereas dogs see humans as part of their pack and a resource to aid them in solving problems.

When we lived in Chattanooga, we bred our female GSD Heidi. It was winter time and we had Heidi's whelping box in the garage with a kerosene heater to provide warmth. One evening, there was a rap on the back door leading to the garage. When I opened the door, there stood Heidi. She walked over to the heater, then to the kerosene container and then back to me. The heater had run out of fuel and she needed me to refuel and relight the heater. I wish I was as good a communicator as Heidi!

In Alexandra Horowitz's book *Inside of a Dog*, she mentions several similar stories of dogs using humans as a resource to solve a problem. Humans and dogs were just meant to be and work together. Maybe one of the reasons we love our dogs so much is they help us become a better person – the person we were meant to be.

Dogs have made a lot of strides in my lifetime. In Vietnam and earlier wars, military dogs were regarded as "equipment" and were left in country with the rest of the equipment. Today they are regarded as soldiers, and efforts are made to have them adopted after their military service – as it should be. After meeting and being around Dollar, I cannot imagine him being abandoned. Today he is a happy pet, toting around his toy and wanting someone to give him some attention.

It used to be common practice to have dogs kept outside on a chain, and in many circles today that is considered animal cruelty. To live a "dogs' life" is definitely getting better.

One of the reasons this is a good book for leadership is that a dog is always going to be testing to ensure someone is the leader. If you and other family members are not providing the leadership then the dogs will. A home where the dog is the leader is not as happy as it could be if the human took on that responsibility. Chaos reigns if the dog is the leader in the house. My friend Wes Jenson also sells working line German Shepherds. I was at his place one afternoon when a lady was returning her dog to Wes, and she was in tears. The dog was about 18 months old and she loved her dog. However, it was obvious that she had not provided the leadership for this very powerful and dominant dog and in the dogs mind, he was the leader. He had bitten the woman twice, and it was just more dog for her than she could handle so she had to give it up. Thank heavens she took the dog back to Wes so that he could find it a home where they would provide the needed leadership for this dog. Many people would have taken the dog to the Humane Society and it would have been put down for being a "mean dog." I am certain today that this dog is a well-mannered pet.

Dogs are master manipulators of their environment to get what they want, and they are opportunistic predators, which translates to "do not leave your pot roast unattended." They will not lie to you and if they have an ego, it does not seem to get in the way. Your dog may try and hoodwink you into giving him what he wants, but they will be honest about it. So – if you and the dog are having a relationship problem or a work related problem it is your fault. Somewhere along the line your leadership failed. That is one of the reasons this book is hard to write as it exposes many of my own faults.

Dogs have no sense of tomorrow nor do they care much about yesterday – it is all about right now. We need to strive to be more like them. Your dog wants to be with you now and you would be well advised to listen to him – one day in the future he will not be there and will be nothing more than a memory. Can we learn to "be with" those we lead and love right now before it is too late and we have regrets?

I was walking past a lacrosse game at our local school. The kids were probably 9-11 years old and parents were there to watch. I noticed one dad had his head down looking at his smart phone. I just stopped and observed for a few minutes. The man never lifted his head. I finally tapped him on the shoulder and asked him if he had a child in the game and he said he did. I told him that his son observed what I saw – a dad that was not there. That dad needs to learn how to "be there."

We all like to have someone to blame for our shortcomings. Our pastor was telling a story about a single mom who was headed to bed for the evening. As she walked down the hallway she saw candy wrappers. She followed the trail of candy wrappers to her little girl's room where there was a huge pile of the wrappers. When she asked her daughter about the wrappers the little girl answered, "I didn't do it mom." The mom replied, "Sweetie, there are only two people who live here – you and me, and I did not do it." The little girl sighed and said, "I wished I had a little brother." Many times, we all wish we had a little brother to blame our shortcomings on. There are no little brothers when working with dogs.

When we are leading people and something goes wrong we can sometimes rationalize that the other person is messed up; somehow they are to fault for our failed effort. With you and the dog – it is on you. That is why studying our leadership style with dogs may be so effective. When something goes wrong   in human-human leadership situations, it is still your fault but it is not as easy to see. Did you make a bad hire? Did you provide inadequate training? Did you not have a good relationship? Somewhere it is on you. Now, don't feel too down on yourself as you are not alone in being the "not so perfect leader." We all have growing to do and it is a moving target. Let's just try and be better today than we were yesterday.

I recently read an article in the Washington Post relating that people grieve just as hard, or perhaps harder, for their dogs than they do people. Several explanations were given. One explanation was that our dogs are totally dependent on us (that dominion thing again) and thus we second-guess ourselves on whether or not we have done a good job for them; there is an element of guilt. What if we felt as bad and guilty when our leadership actions failed our team? Would we do better the next time?

I do not know the author but I love the prayer that says, "Help me O Lord, become the person my dog believes I am."

Dogs and people are meant to be in relationships. They are not like a TV set where you can turn them on and off. You must be with them in the moment. When Fido comes and nudges your arm to play with him while you are working on your computer, go ahead and stop. Take time to enjoy the moment and be in the relationship. Relationships are established by moments in time, so we must engage.

This is one of the areas where it gets difficult for me to write this as I am not so certain that I do a good job at this with people. Do I spend as much time on real relationships with those that I directly lead? Probably not. Would things get better if I did? Yes.

We owe both the dogs and the people we lead our time and effort to strengthen the relationship. We must start by making it a priority in which we dedicate our most precious resource – our time. The gift of time is the gift of love. We must make time.

The purpose of making time for relationships is not for you, your dog, and your employees to go skipping through the tulips singing kumbaya. The main purpose is for information flow – information flows through relationships, and the processes we employ in our work and personal lives needs and feeds off of information.

Let's consider a business example of the relationship between a sales person and a plant manager. The sales person gains information from the field that there is a defect in the product. The information flow between the sales person and one working in the plant is critical if the problem is to get solved in a timely manner. However what if the salesman considers the plant manager to be only concerned about production volume and not concerned about customers? And what if the plant manager considered the salesmen's life style of fancy clothes and several rounds of golf each week a bit extravagant? If those two perceptions persist, what are the chances of good information flow through their relationship? If neither sales person nor plant person took the time to establish a decent relationship, it would adversely affect the performance of the company.

In summary, what should we have learned from this chapter? The issue of dominion is huge – each of us have an enormous responsibility to treat our surroundings and the people and creatures in that surrounding with honor and respect. We may disrupt the environment, but we must honor those in the environment.

We also learned about the tight knit working relationships with dogs and people. The exact same thing is true for people and people, but sometimes we take that for granted.

We learned that the dog is a great laboratory for us to practice self-reflection as it relates to our leadership style and ability. Our dogs are not as complex and many times our actions have an immediate effect that we can observe and learn from. It is also great for us to serve our dogs as it helps teach humility. Most

U.S. Presidents in my lifetime have owned a dog. I hope they are the ones that scoop up the dog poop and feed Fido. This type of action serves to enhance our servant leadership skills. I like that in a president.

One of the most valuable things we can give our people and dogs is our time, and being there emotionally when you are there physically.

We learned that the primary benefit of strong relationships is good information flow through those relationships.

Chapter Three

House Breaking Your Puppies and Your Employees

"Maggie NO!" I screamed as I scooped her up just as she was squatting to relieve herself on the carpet. It is all part of puppy training. She of course was shaken by my sudden reaction which was my intent. I wanted her to understand that I was upset. We continued outside and I gently placed her in the area where we would like for her to go to the bathroom. Ears back and with relief in her eyes she finished her business. "Good girl, good girl," I praised her up and made a big deal out of how good she was. You could almost see the joy in her eyes of getting this positive attention. After a little playing outside we came back in the house. I made a note to myself to increase the frequency of trips outside to the potty.

Today, a five year old Maggie would burst a bladder before she would pee on the carpet. When the urge strikes she goes to the door, or whatever it takes to get either Linda or me off our butt to let her outside.

Let's see if we can translate this house breaking exercise into a business leadership learning experience.

We were in a meeting with our largest client in our conference room. Attending was their CEO, president, and other members of their ownership team. We were going through project plans and suddenly I noticed our new 20-something year old employee (one of our puppies) squatting to pee on the conference room carpet. Actually, she had her head down texting (the equivalent of peeing in our world). I wanted to shout "Brenda NO!" and then scoop her up and take her outside to finish her texting.

We had recently hired two relatively young college graduates and it finally dawned on me that our company was not equipped to train puppies. Dogs that come into our company need to already be house-trained and field-tested. We do not have the capacity and expertise to train puppies. Brenda and the other puppy we hired now work for other, larger companies, which is good for them and good for us.

My first jobs were with the US Navy and DuPont. The Navy and DuPont are excellent at training puppies. These massive organizations routinely bring in young recruits, officer candidates, and recent college graduates in masse. These puppies have other pups to learn from and play with plus there are some young people with a few years of experience to help guide them along. I learned things in both organizations that I would not have learned in smaller organizations because these organizations were equipped to handle this knowledge transfer and experience, giving it in a systematic method. General Electric is another organization that has a reputation for training young recruits and developing them into good business leaders. They do such a good job that they have more than they need and many leave GE to go head other organizations. In the Navy and at DuPont there were endless courses on everything from how to write better, firefighting, goal setting, quality programs, and the list could go on and on. Also, there were plenty of old salts and old dogs that would quickly correct a young pup that started to pee on the rug or have their head down texting in an important client meeting.

When I was telling my dog peeing on the carpet story to my good friend Milton Davis, he laughed. Milton is a sales executive with a very large engineering construction firm and they hire and train pups. They also have a mentoring program and Milton is a mentor. He was relating a story of taking his mentee out to lunch, and during the lunch his mentee took out his smart phone and began to text. "What are you doing?" Milton asked. "I thought we discussed that it was rude to text while with someone." The mentee replied, "Well it's only you." Milton wanted to pick him up by the scruff of the neck and shake him like a mama dog but a quick verbal reprimand got the job done.

When you raise a dog from a puppy and keep it through death there are several distinct phases that you and the dog go through together. Your leadership and management methods will change as time together progresses. This is just out of necessity. I do not provide the same sort of leadership to my daughter now that I did when she was seven years old. Our relationship has changed, thus the way we interact has changed. The same is true with your employees and your dog.

When you first get that bundle of fur you have a lot of ground work to do. Life should be full of play and learning to accept your leadership.

Later in the book we are going to spend time talking about selection of dogs and employees. Putting a bracket on experience for a firm is probably a good first step that we had not thought of until now. I doubt that we will hire any new college graduates unless our business model changes significantly.

Getting a new puppy to maturity takes a lot of work, patience, knowledge, and love. When we get done, we want a dog that does not eat your shoe, can sit, down, heel, come, and perhaps stay. We want the dog not to jump up on our friends (go ahead and maul those enemies), does not steal your roast beef off the stove, and respects you as the leader of the pack. Dog trainer Wes Jenson says that there are three basic phases to your relationship with your dog – up to six months when they are a pure puppy. Again, this time should be full of fun which can also mean training. Phase two, six months to two years – some really serious training including learning how to deal with stress happens in this phase. During this time dogs are almost like teenagers – they can be a pain in the rear and some handlers will not put a dog in a competitive trial until they are older than two years for fear they may run off the field to chase a squirrel. After two years – kick back and enjoy your dog. As a dog lover, I am going to take a small pause here. There is another phase as well, and that is when your dog gets old and grey and they need a lot of special attention. There is a special place in hell for those people who take their old dogs to the humane society to die.

When Maggie was a young dog, I would always run into Bob and his golden lab, Abby, at the school in the mornings. We would always talk. Abby was getting older and not quite as spry, but she still loved her walks with Bob. As several years went by Bob would just take Abby up to the school and sit with her. Bob had explained that he and his wife had gotten Abby shortly after they had married – they had no children and Abby was essentially their child. One day Bob stopped showing up. Shortly after the time Bob stopped coming to the school, I walked by his house and he was outside. I stopped and talked and he told me that it had finally come that time for Abby and she was now over the Rainbow Bridge – she had died. Bob was devastated, but he did the right thing by Abby. Abby ended her life with her friend by her side and left knowing that she was loved. That is the way you do it.

Dogs that will eventually be seeing eye dogs are sent to foster homes when they are puppies to get socialized and obtain general obedience. When they get to a certain age they go off to learn their specialized skill and then are paired with their blind owners. The seeing eye group is not geared up to train puppies so they farm that task out to others. Essentially that is what we will do at Chesapeake Consulting.

At what point in this process is your organization?

My first industrial job was with DuPont. At my plant location they hired only chemical engineers from specific universities and they wanted the top 10% of the class. That was how they selected the pups they would train. Each of us young pups had a mentor. When I look back, they put a lot of effort and money into training young pups (and older dogs for that matter). Many of these large companies do such an excellent job of training pups that they end up providing leaders for other, smaller firms. Sometimes large firms do not present the opportunities for advancement and challenge, so their trained pups go to hunt with different owners, I know that was the case with me and DuPont. They expect and plan for that fallout.

Brenda, our texting young pup, has since left our company because she also understood that we were not prepared to train puppies and she was wise enough to know she needed training. I know Brenda will eventually read this book and recognize herself. In essence, we purchased a very high pedigreed puppy without the knowledge on how to raise it. It was a huge learning experience for us and will allow us to improve our focus on our employment efforts in the future. What we do best is bring in some high achieving people that have little or no need for even a leash correction. We allow them to be themselves with very little rules. We want these high achievers to be able to make a difference unencumbered by hogwash. With young pups, a certain amount of hogwash is necessary to get them to the training level needed to be productive.

The leadership lesson is this – bringing employees into your organization and preparing them to help your company may be the most important task you perform as a leader. There is a science and process to this task and the wise leader understands this process relative to their organization. I did not do a good job as a leader with Brenda. The fact of the matter is we are not geared up to bring on board new college graduates and provide them with the experiences they need to be ultra-successful in the business world. What has changed by writing this book is now we understand this. Education and knowledge transfer is one of your most important functions as a leader. All this knowledge came from the dog.

Chapter Four

How to Select Dogs and People; Is It the Same?

It was down to two job candidates for the sales position we had open. The gentleman we were interviewing was not like the rest of us. He dressed a little different and none of us really warmed up to him, although the battery of tests we had given each candidate indicated this was the fellow we should hire. We just were not comfortable with him. On the other hand, the next candidate was ideal. He was a Naval Academy graduate and had an advanced business degree from a prestigious university. He was more like us. We laughed during the interview and everyone felt grand about this fellow, although the same battery of tests said this guy was not going to be suitable in the sales position we were looking to fill. We went with who we liked and hired the Naval Academy guy. After two years, he had not sold one Dime's worth of business and consumed vast resources in going after contracts. There did not appear to be a method to his madness and not only had we not sold anything, we were not close. Everyone still liked him but the hire was a failure. When I let him go, he got violently mad and did not take his termination well. He seemed unable to connect the dots of no sales to loss of sales position.

I guess I never learn my lesson. Not long ago we hired a young MBA graduate that everyone liked. He had a wonderful personality (we translated that into a sales personality). We hired based on need and emotion, not science. At least I discovered earlier that this was another failed hire and I terminated his employment before we got too far down the road. I should have read and adhered to my friend Jerry Bradshaw's advice on selecting working dogs in his book *Controlled Aggression.*

Jerry Bradshaw is the founder and owner of Tar Heel Canine in North Carolina. He wears a backwards baseball cap, tee shirt and shorts all the time except in winter when it is a backwards baseball cap sweat shirt and sweat pants. I think he must sleep in that garb. One of our clients had a need for a security company to guard a very large site. I knew that Jerry had contacts in the field so I recommended him to our client. Jerry was to meet our client in West Virginia, but I was unable to go, so one of our other consultants, Carl Gerhiser went. When Carl returned I asked him – "Please tell me that Jerry Bradshaw did not wear his backwards baseball cap." Carl assured me that Jerry was dressed like a perfect gentleman.

Dog trainers are an odd lot as a group, but Jerry may be odder than most. He has a PhD in economics from the University of North Carolina and got interested in dog training after his apartment was broken into and a friend suggested he get a guard dog. He got a Belgium Malinois and became hooked on training working dogs, mostly Malinois and German Shepherds for the police, other law enforcement, and the military. I have read a lot of dog training books, but I probably gravitate more to Jerry because he is almost a scientist (economics is close) and he takes that approach in developing processes for training dogs – and again my premise is that all of this can be applied to humans.

An important part of Jerry's business is selecting the proper dog. He spends a lot of time in Europe visiting different breeders and testing dogs to get the perfect match for his clients. Dogs that have already obtained Schutzhund titles tell you something about the dogs' ability to work. However Jerry has his own tests that he puts the dogs through. It is cut and dry – if a dog fails the test he does not select that dog regardless of how much he personally likes the dog or the breeder. There is no compromise. I should have Jerry hire my next sales executive.

A mistake in hiring is probably the most expensive one you can make. If you make a poor hire not only are you losing several years salary, but you are also losing opportunity benefits such as increased business and profits if you had made the correct hire. Throw in your management and leadership time and what you could have been getting accomplished if you did not have to stop and address the negative consequences of the bad hire. It is terrible and thus it is certainly worth the effort to do it right the first time.

The first step in selection is to identify the job you want done, and this should be as detailed as possible. What do you want your dog to do – search and rescue, detection of drugs, weapons or explosives, therapy dog, bird hunting, good family companion, or a host of other things. In dogs perhaps your first cycle of elimination would be breed. I say that reluctantly as I have seen some breeds do jobs that I would never have thought possible. In the Covington family, I believe our best Schutzhund dog ever would have been my little buddy Griffin, the Cairn terrier who likes to steal cat food. I credit him with some of Maggie's lack of bite work skills. Part of preparing a dog for bite work is to play tug of war and to build the dogs' confidence. The dog needs to win most of these battles. As a young dog, Maggie would play tug with Griffin and drag him all over the house or yard only to finally give up because Griffin would hold on and tug for dear life. Thank heavens Griffin only weighed 20 pounds. He would have been a holy terror if he had been the size of a shepherd. Having said that, we need to remember that most breeds are bred for a specific job or task and you should learn what that is and how it aligns with your needs.

I have been amazed at the detail that has been developed on selecting dogs. Joachim and Wendy Volhand developed an excellent Puppy Aptitude Test that you can use to select your dog. There are nine test involved and six different responses to look for in each test. Here are a few of the test items to give you a feel for the detail:

A. Clap your hands and call the puppy.
   1. Came with tail up, jumped and bit your hands.
   2. Came tail up, pawed, licked your hands.
   3. Came, tail up.
   4. Came tail down.
   5. Reluctantly came, tail down.
   6. Did not come

B. Stand up, walk away from pup, coax pup to follow.
   1. Followed, tail up, got underfoot and bit your feet.
   2. Followed, tail up, got underfoot.
   3. Followed, tail up.
   4. Followed, tail down.
   5. Reluctantly followed, tail down,
   6. Did not follow.

C. Gently hold pup on its back for 30 seconds.
   1. Struggled, bit, and flailed.
   2. Struggled, flailed
   3. Struggled, settled, struggled, with some eye contact
   4. Struggled, then settled.
   5. No struggle
   6. No struggle, no eye contact

Here is how they analyze the tests:

1. Mostly ones are dogs that are very dominant, aggressive and have high fight drive. Would require a very experienced handler and not a good dog for most individuals. A good guard dog and/or some police work.
2. Mostly twos are dominant and self-assured. Have high fight drive and also needs someone comfortable around working dogs. Good competitive dog and family dog for those who know what they are doing.
3. Mostly threes are outgoing and friendly. May be too much dog for elderly or family with small children.

4. Mostly fours are easily controlled, submissive and high pack drive. Easy to train, self-confident and makes wonderful family pet.
5. Mostly fives are extremely submissive, bonds very close with owner, needs predictable home life. Need owners that are not over demanding.
6. Mostly sixes are independent, low in pack drive and are uninterested in people. This is very rare.

If you are interested in getting the entire test it is copyrighted by Wendy Volhard in 2002 and is called *Puppy Aptitude Test*.

The next time you have a job candidate, you will want to have them lay on their back, hold them down for 30 seconds, and see how they behave. That might not be a good idea. However the science of testing behavior as a predictor of future behavior is certainly valid. If you do not have good prior knowledge of a job candidate and you fail to test them then you are taking a large risk for your organization. The tests are not fool proof but you are at least making an effort to put more science into the hiring process.

I attended an advanced tracking class at Tar Heel Canine, given by Ono Bren, an expert in the field from the Netherlands. Ono mentioned that tracking is the hardest thing for a dog to do both mentally and physically. He reviewed criteria for both dogs and handlers. For dogs they needed to have no aggression, good prey drive, a drive to search, and motivation to work, even in bad conditions. They must also have good social character. All of this can be tested for. In handlers (the leader), he wants patience and perseverance.

There are a variety of psychology test that one can administer to test humans for particular jobs. The ones we employ are the success insights executive DISC which measures behavior based on the four dimensions of dominance, influence, steadiness, and compliance; Workplace Motivators which measures the relative prominence of several basic motivators, and Personal Talent and

Skills Index which determines how one views the world around them and gets into practical thinking and systems judgment.

In *Controlled Aggression*, Bradshaw talks about almost similar evaluations for dogs as we have for humans. Bradshaw describes public sociability and the ability to adapt to change. We test humans for the same thing. He talks about different drives in dogs which can assist in determining what motivates the dog. The same is critical for humans. If someone is not motivated by money and that is how you are trying to motivate them, you will fail.

I have given a few bad examples of how I messed up in hiring people, but let me also hit on a couple of success stories. Note that on the success stories, there is some actual reasoning behind the decisions other than emotions and whether or not I like someone. Within our first decade of being in business, we had a great administrative team – Melanie Morinze and Liz Judy, who is our current controller. They both filled their particular roles great and our office ran like clockwork. As luck would have it, Melanie fell in love and that sorry rascal that she was marrying had the gall to move Melanie to Texas to live with him. How inconsiderate! Before Melanie got married and left, we began working to find her replacement. We wanted an exact Xerox copy of Melanie. The first step was to interview and dissect Melanie to see what made her click so we could enhance the chances of getting her clone. After interviewing her, we made up a list of interview questions that we would add to the normal interview questions. Joann Rupert was one of the job candidates for the job. Some of the questions on the interview were:

1. If you ordered a steak medium rare and it came out medium what would you do? (Melanie's answer – "nothing")
2. Tell me your favorite type of music. (Melanie's answer – "country")
3. Tell me how your house gets decorated during the holiday season. (Melanie's answer—"I do it all myself.")

When Joann left the interview we were all excited that we felt we had found the next Melanie. Joann went home and told her family that she really liked the company that she interviewed for but they really asked weird questions and she was afraid she bombed the interview. We hired Joann and she was perfect. During the transition period Joann worked alongside Melanie and they laughed concerning how much alike they were. The end results were that Joann ended up working 15 years and retired at Chesapeake. The test we gave Joann was crude, but was effective. However a word of caution on interview questions – note how question three did not specify which holiday. Had it been a specific religious holiday some would probably say it was an unfair question. However these questions are not unlike questions in many behavioral assessments that are standard in hiring methods today.

Another thing that I did that worked was only hire people that had gone through what I called "screening organizations." A screening organization is one that is very selective and perhaps demanding. What I was doing there was taking advantage of their Human Resources and selection organizations. Service academies are screening organizations (although I obviously had one bad apple on that). They used to be extremely selective and had a rigorous engineering curriculum. DuPont, Monsanto, Dow, General Motors, Ford, etc., are other such organizations.

Recently one of the more eye opening discoveries has been learning about the theories in requisite organizations, an approach developed by Elliott Jacques at the turn of the last century. Jacques claims that every job has a time span component to it. For example, a machine operator has a time span of about 4-8 hours. We give the operator a job and when he completes it, he comes to get another job with an accompanying set of instructions. An area supervisor may need a time span of a week. He may need to develop a weekly schedule for several machines and operators and perhaps schedule a safety meeting for his team – a bit more complex.

A plant manager may need a time span of 18 to 24 months as there are budgets to prepare investment plans, new product introductions, etc. A CEO may need a time span of 5-10 years. Jacques claims there are seven levels of time spans, so incorporating this in a job specification would be important.

Now, each person has a time span capability and it has nothing to do with education. One of the best ways to determine time span capability is to note projects one has worked on in the past. The young MBA grad that I mentioned had a time span problem, which by the way is unfixable. Some people are able to increase their time span capability with age, but that is certainly not worth waiting around for. The job he was in required a time span of 18 to 24 months and his demonstrated time span was much less than that. He was a nice kid that never quite understood why we let him go, but that was it. It was my fault by not understanding and checking with this in the beginning.

I *think* I have seen the same thing in dogs. On July 4, 2010 it was hotter than the dickens. Maggie and I got called to do a search in northern Virginia as two Labradors were missing. Part of the search was through neighborhoods and part was through woods. We were out there for 2 hours in heat of over 100 degrees. Of course we took water breaks, but Maggie did not miss a beat with respect to working and doing her job. I think that is about all the time span I could have expected. I have been around a lot of other dogs that I know would have not kept their concentration for that period of time. Border Collies as a breed appear to have a high time span.

A time span is essentially the time someone can go without being supervised. Why is this important? Obviously if we have someone in a position that requires a certain time span and they do not have that capability, the job will not get done properly. If we have someone with a very high time span capability and we have them in a position that requires a low time span, then there is the danger of them getting bored, especially if they have not filled that capacity void with meaningful out of work activities such as charity work or a hobby. I have run across some unhappy Border Collie owners that did not engage their dogs – if you do not give a Border Collie something to do they will invent something; like dismantling your house.

Time span in the selection of people and dogs is relatively new. Proponents say it has a higher correlation of success of any other method. I personally do not know – however it is intriguing enough for me to continue the research.

What are we learning here from a leadership perspective? We are learning to keep focused on assessments that demonstrate one's talent or aptitude for a particular job as the core. I have run into a lot of companies that like to do "cultural interviews" which involve trying to determine the "fit" of someone to the company culture. Some go so far as to say that is the only thing they look at as they can train the needed skills. I think that is a huge mistake. There is nothing wrong with the cultural interview; however do those interviews on a subset of people who you have already determined can do the job. It is pure arrogance to think you can train any person to do a specific job. Use your gut feeling and whether or not you like someone as a secondary selection criterion. I am sure that it is possible to hire one that is qualified and that everyone likes. The main objective here is to not make the "everyone likes them" the number one criteria in job selection, and that is difficult not to do. Take it from experience.

Chapter Five

The Power of Focus – Get Better Results

Maggie and I were out for our morning walk an approaching was a lady walking two dogs; one of which was snarling and tugging at its leash to get at us. Maggie's back braced up and she stared at the oncoming situation. She gave quick glances up to me to see if all was okay. She didn't growl, snarl, or lunge – just an observant stare as we approached. After we passed, Maggie went into a pretty competitive heel (fus in German) with her head turned up at me and looking into my eyes. She seemed to have a smile on her face as if to say "Did I do good Daddy? Huh, did I do good?" Yes she did and she got some sort of reward, either a dog treat, a little roughhouse rub, a pat on the side, or simple just telling her what a good girl she is.

It wasn't too many years ago that Maggie was on the edge of being dog aggressive. Not long after we had gotten Maggie, my daughter's Basset Hound (Abigail) attacked the small pup. It was our fault for not paying closer attention and the vet said not to worry, that Maggie would even the score. Oh did she ever even the score to the tune of a $500 vet bill to repair Abigail after Maggie cleaned her clock over a dispute involving a ball. I have since learned that on some occasions an event like being attacked as a puppy can lead to dog aggression. Maggie was on the way there. That was a problem that needed to be resolved. Aggression by your dog reflects on your leadership. Your dog should never fight unless you say it is okay – you are the leader.

Your dog may test your leadership in two ways: will your dog freely give you one of their treasured assets such as a toy or food and will your dog obey your commands in time of stress. An oncoming dog snarling and jerking at the leash could be a stressful situation for your dog; will your dog obey your command during this event? That is one of the many reasons obedience training for your dog is so important; you can give your dog an alternative action in times they may get themselves and/or you in trouble.

One of the things you should teach your dog is to look into your eyes on command --- to focus on your face. In the research for this book, I have learned how important eye contact is as a communications technique. "Your eye is the lamp of your body. When your eye is good, your whole body also is full of light. But when they are bad, your body is also full of darkness." Luke 11:34.

I know that the importance of eye contact is true for a dog and it is probably true for people. You communicate many emotions with your eyes; I know when Linda gives me "that look" that I had best mind my P's and Q's. Several of the dog trainers I studied were adamant about making strong eye contact. However you first must be able to get the dog to look into your eyes.

I do several things with Maggie to teach and encourage eye contact. Spitting hotdogs at her is my most favorite method which also confirms to my wife that I am crazy. What I do is get some hotdog bits in my mouth, have Maggie on a short leash in front of me, and spit the hotdogs towards her face. If she fails to catch the hotdog, I use the leash to prevent her from getting it off the ground. If she fails to catch it, she misses the treat. Another is to have her sit in front of me while I have a treat in each hand and my hands are held out to my sides. She does not get the treat if she looks at my hands, only when she stays focused on my eyes will I give her the reward. Spitting hotdogs is also a neat technique to teach competitive heeling. My suggestion is to get a brand of hotdogs that you like – there is nothing wrong with the handler getting a treat once in a while.

When we are walking and I give the command "eyes," I expect for her to turn her head and gaze at me until I release her from the command. We began working on her dog aggression by having her look into my eyes whenever another dog approached and when the dog passed and she was obedient, we made a big deal out of it. If she tried to turn towards the dog she would get a quick yank on the leash and a "nope!" Problem is now solved. Today I do not even give the "eye" command. I let her look at the oncoming dog and she never reacts in a poor manner. The other owner is always amazed at how laid back Maggie is. Of course, what they do not see is that after we pass Maggie pops that head around expecting some sort of "atta girl" from me, which she always gets.

I actually think this is a good lesson here as Maggie respects my leadership on this and she buys into the process. Other dogs are not as important to Maggie as her relationship with me. She gets it and now there is no effort required. I trust her to behave herself and be okay with other dogs. That does not mean she will not let a rude dog know right quick to back off and stay out of her area and that is okay. I know she is not going to bite them. It all started with the power to focus on my eyes and keep that focus.

The basis of CCI's consulting practice is the Theory of Constraints (TOC). The idea behind TOC is that all complex systems have very few leverage points that can have a huge impact on performance. Each one in the organization needs to focus on their role in constraint management for the organization to reach its maximum capability.

Linda and I came to the Baltimore area when I was hired to run the Sherwin-Williams plant. The plant was performing poorly and my job was to turn it around. One of the many problems with the site was that it was not producing enough paint. There are several steps in the manufacturing process of paint but the one that was constraining this particular facility was the grinding operation. We were able to increase overall volume out of the plant by nearly 30% with no capital expenditures just by having everyone focus on maximizing the output of grinding. Processes downstream of grinding made sure that grinding always had empty tanks to pump to, otherwise grinding would have to stop producing. Processes upstream of grinding made sure grinding did not shut down because of lack of raw materials and workers. The power of focus turned that particular plant around from the worst performing facility to the best in less than two years. These results saved several hundred jobs in the Baltimore area as that plant was previously being considered for elimination.

The leadership message is to stay focused on those few things that are the most important issues at the time. You want to keep your nose down and your tail up.

Because we are talking about focus, I am going to put in a plug for people embracing TOC as an approach to management. TOC has been around since the 1980's and really took off in popularity in the 1990's. There is a lot of power to the five steps of TOC. Initially, one must define the system they want to analyze and its' purpose and how you measure success. Then:

1. Identify the system's constraint.
2. Decide how to exploit the system's constraint.
3. Subordinate all to the above decisions
4. Do not let inertia become the system's constraint.
5. Go back to step one.

If you have an interest in learning more about the Theory of Constraints, I would recommend reading the book *The Goal*, by Eli Goldratt.

In all complex systems (your organization, family, etc.), the items in the system are interconnected. Also, at any given time there is one of those items that is the leverage point of the system, and if that is where attention is focused, the system will experience enormous improvement and success.

Let me give you a quick example. In most hospitals, the operating room is the item that makes the most money for the hospital – get more people through the operating room and you make more money. However, much of the time an operating room spends is idle time because it is not ready for the next surgery. Many hospital administrators are convinced they need more operating rooms so they try and raise capital to do so. However, the problem of the operating room not being ready is normally due to not having supplies, nurses, or people to get the room cleaned and prepared. Simple changes in policy, hiring practices, and scheduling (actions to exploit the constraint) would result in enormous profit increases for the hospital and perhaps keep medical cost down for us all. That means you should give a copy of this book to your local hospital.

The leadership lesson is to stay focused on the task at hand – easy to say, more difficult to actually do. Many of us have a tendency to multi-task. When multi-tasking, we actually prolong the overall length to complete assignments. Try to be in the moment – focus on the task at hand then when complete, move to the next moment and task.

Chapter Six

In Order to Focus, We Must Learn to Trust

For several weeks Janet has been working with us on drug detection. Normally Janet is super nice and easy on Maggie and me. On this particular day, we must have progressed to the point where the honeymoon was over. Looking back on the situation, I believe Janet felt Maggie had the drug thing down pat and now she needed to work on the stupid one of the team – me.

We normally do three searches, one each with marijuana, cocaine, and heroin. The first search of the day was near a cabana close to a tree line, and after Janet coaxing and telling me where to search, we found the stuff. The next search was a car where there were no drugs and then one where there was. Janet was encouraging me to watch for what Maggie was telling me. She did not appear to be focused on Maggie at all. Normally when Maggie finds the drugs, Janet throws Maggie's ball at the spot where she found the drugs and we have a little play session. We proceeded to the next station which was an open air bus stop. You know the type – covered, bench and sides that are about 10 inches off the ground. Janet said the drugs were in or around the bus stop. Maggie quickly went past the adjacent trash container to the left side of the bench inside the bus stop. Her nose went to the corner and it looked like she had found the loot – but sneaky Janet did not throw the ball. What's the deal? I pulled Maggie outside the bus stop and we went around the back, and when Maggie got to that corner she poked her nose under the 10 inch gap up towards that bench again and she was quite adamant. Still Janet did not throw the ball. We went back inside the bus stop and Maggie pulled me over to that corner again. I started to move a paper cup to look myself and Janet yells – "What are you doing?" I replied that I was looking for the drugs. Janet retorted that Maggie was supposed to be looking for the drugs and I was supposed to be focused on Maggie --- not the drugs. She then asked, "Oh by the way, what do you think?" I told her I thought the drugs were in that corner. She said, "you are correct" and then tossed the ball. What Janet was looking for was for me to be focused on the dog and then give my answer based on what I saw; she wanted me to have confidence in what my dog was telling me. We were not done with the session, even though we had done the three searches. Janet said she had one more place she wanted us to search, and that was a shed. Maggie and I went around the shed two times like Janet had instructed and Maggie was not indicating anything. Again, Janet stood there with her arms crossed observing. I then said to Janet, "I do not think there are any drugs here." She asked why I thought that and I replied and said that Maggie did not indicate any. She then smiled like the satisfied teacher and beamed, "You're right!"

Stay focused on your role and your job. Staying focused on your job and not everyone else's job is another exercise in trust. Whenever I observe a leader that appears totally out of control and has effectiveness problems, part of the problem is not being able to accomplish this task of focus and trust.

A lady in the western part of Baltimore lost her dog and Maggie and I were called to help. The way this works is the pet owner supplies us with a scent item – something that smells like their pet such as a bed, blanket, or toy. Maggie smelled the item and that told her what she was looking for. After she was scented up, Maggie wanted to go into the owners' back yard. I am thinking to myself, "Of COURSE the scent is going to be in the dogs own back yard, but I appeased Maggie and we went there anyway." Once in the back yard Maggie pulled me over to a parked camper. However, the door on the camper was shut so there is no way the lost dog was in the camper so I pulled her away. Maggie pulled me back to the camper and I pulled her away a second time. She turned around, gave me a disgusted look (dogs can give you a disgusted look) and she took a poop in the lady's yard, which I had to stop and clean up. We then went off tracking all over the neighborhood, through a graveyard (it was now getting dark), and some woods and eventually back to the lady's house. I left her with some instructions on checking with the Humane Society and told her to call me if she had a sighting of her dog, and that Maggie and I would come back. The next day, my friend Anne Wills called and asked, "Did you see a camper in the back yard?" I replied, "Well yes, as a matter of fact Maggie kept trying to take me there." Anne gave her trademark belly laugh and said --- "Well that is where the dog was; you should have listened to Maggie!" Aah!!

What had happened was the dog had jumped the fence, roamed all over the neighborhood, came back and jumped back in the yard, and walked in the camper when the door was open. The owner saw the door on her camper open and shut it, locking the dog inside. Fortunately, she went to show a neighbor the camper and out came the dog. Janet's voice rang in my ear; "Trust your dog."

When I am riding on an airplane I trust the pilot to get me to my destination safely and I can focus on whatever it is I am working on during the flight. However if I knew more about flying, I might find myself second guessing the pilot to the point of being distracted from my task. I assume and trust that the pilot knows what he is doing. The trouble with trust and focus seems to arise when we do not have total confidence and/or we think we can do it better. I thought I knew better than Maggie on the search. I had reasoned there was no way that dog could have been in that trailer – I was wrong. The reason we failed on this mission was I was not focused on reading what she was telling me – I was too busy figuring out where the lost dog was and that was not my job; that was Maggie's job.

The same thing can happen at work. I trust the employees at Chesapeake Consulting and since I do, I am able to focus on a variety of things that I want to do – such as writing this book.

In the early 1980's I accepted a job as Vice-President of Operations for Gilman Paint Company in Chattanooga, Tennessee. The job involved providing leadership for all areas of the company except sales, finance, and research. Jim Tisheaur, who was a plant manager, reported to me. Jim was in his early 60's at the time, had a chemistry degree from the University of Louisville, and had been in the paint industry all of his life. The company was building an office for me and they had told Jim that he had to vacate his office until mine was complete. He had already moved to a much smaller office (looked like a closet) before I had arrived. My first action was to order Jim to move back into his office and give me the closet. I told him a few months in a closet would do me good. There were also a lot of suggestions from some of my peers who had been at Gilman a long time that Jim was a major problem with manufacturing and that he should be terminated. I normally ignore such suggestions as I prefer to make up my own mind. I quickly learned that I could trust Jim in many ways, including the technical details on paint manufacturing. I was more knowledgeable on progressive leadership and manufacturing techniques for a plant so we made a great team. In a short period of time, the operations side of the business which had been a problem became the company's competitive edge and a source of pride. Our company was recognized locally and nationally for such things as safety records and innovative management processes. Being able to trust Jim Tisheaur was a large part of that success, allowing me to focus on issues that I was good at. It was my choice as to whether or not to trust Jim. Although he was nearly 30 years older than me, we became great friends.

Recently I was talking with one of my neighbors and he was telling me about his wife having a hard time at work, and that she had received a reprimand. Sue was very good at her job, but there was some miscommunication on a proposal. Instead of addressing the communications problem (which the boss created by the way), the boss takes it out on Sue. I told my friend – so an information flow problem caused the issue, and the boss thinks it is a good idea to harm the relationship between him and Sue (information travels through relationships) so now the information flow will be even worse --- brilliant. The boss needs his prong collar yanked. What the boss should have done was to form the conversation in a manner that both explored what happened AND served to improve or maintain the relationship with Sue. Then there would have been progress relative to the goal of the organization.

There is a word of caution on trust and dominion. If you are the owner of the system or head of the company, you are still responsible for dominion regardless of how much you trust and delegate authority to others. This is fine as long as everyone is still on the same sheet of music. There was a point in our history at CCI where we had one very strong personality wanted to go 100% as a Lean Consulting firm and the another very strong personality wanted to go 100% into Theory of Constraints as taught by the purest. I was uncomfortable with either of those approaches; however I did not step in and give even a leash correction to the ongoing debate. People ended up taking sides, and for the first time in our history we had some nasty internal politics – the very thing I despised about places I had worked before. I even told Linda that if I could I would leave the company, but that was not possible since I was the owner. Eventually the strong personalities left and our culture recovered. The lesson I learned is that in addition to trust, the person in charge of dominion needs to make sure the purpose and vision are clear and understood by all.

Leadership lesson --- trust your dog; trust your people. Relationships are built on trust and information flows through relationships. You simply must trust your dog and your folks. If you cannot trust your dog, you either need to get a new dog or take a really hard look at your own attitude. I would suggest learning to trust your dog as a first step. You will get more accomplished if you focus rather than multitask. In order to stay focused on what you need to do, it is imperative that you trust others to do their job.

Chapter Seven

Your State of Mind Affects Your Dog and Your People

Maggie was working on her elements for Schutzhund obedience which included jumping over a hurdle to retrieve a dumbbell and going up and over an A-frame for a dumbbell. Wes was the instructor and is a great guy with a wonderful sense of humor. The prior week, Maggie had done an excellent job retrieving the dumbbells by going over the hurdle and A-frame. However this week she seemed a little lethargic. I felt it necessary to make an excuse for her; "Maggie seems to be having a bad day." Wes quickly retorted, "Maggie is not having a bad day – YOU are having a bad day and transmitting your crappy attitude to her," and being the nice guy that he is he followed that with a laugh.

This was not the first time I had heard this criticism. Charlie Radle also expressed this concern during several training sessions, "John, liven up a little and make it exciting for your dog. She will take on your level of enthusiasm."

I guess I am relatively low key and normally lack a lot of emotion; that is who I am – but if I want to get my dog fired up, I had better get fired up and be genuine about it as you cannot fool your dog. If I want better results, I must adapt my own behavior and attitude as my feelings are contagious.

This state of mind thing is one of the most important subjects that decent leaders need to address. If things are really going bad (and if you have ever had any level of significant responsibility that will happen), you of all people need to portray a positive image and it needs to be genuine. Other people will feed off of your energy whether it is good or bad energy. Emotion is so strong that some people claim you can smell it. You can bet your dog can smell those emotions. Here is an example of smelling emotions.

Occasionally our alarm system goes off at the office and, as a routine, I travel to the office to meet the police. One time I got there ahead of the police and Maggie and I were coming out of the building at the same time the police officers arrived. What the police officers saw was someone leaving a building, but did not see me as the owner of the building. They were tense and approached me with caution. Maggie went absolutely nuts. She was barking, snarling, and doing everything in her power to let the police officers know to move back. It was all I could do to hold her and keep her from bolting towards the police officers. I yelled that I was going to put her back in the building. I did and then produced an ID so the police knew that I was not the bad guy. The police officers had not said anything nor did they act aggressive – just their tense and cautious attitude was what set Maggie off.

Today, I use Maggie as a demonstration dog when I am teaching the elements to the AKC Good Citizenship test. I call her out to the center and in a very lethargic manner, I ask her to sit, and then to down. She does it, but not very fast – it is actually funny how slow she goes. Then I instantly change my attitude to excited and give the same commands, which she executes immediately and is excited to do them. It is really a cool way to demonstrate to the class the impact of the leaders' state of mind on performance. The major point here is the same thing happens with humans but it is just not so obvious and easy to demonstrate.

Your dog training can be affected by the fight you just had with your spouse or the news that your son just got suspended from school. A keen self-awareness, which is the essence of good leadership, is required for you to determine your own state of mind and to take measures to adapt your mindset to get the most out of the current moment. That is tough to do but necessary if you really want to excel as a leader.

The state of mind thing also goes along with how you feel about people surrounding you. If you do not trust someone, then the relationship is not what is needed and information flows through relationships. The important thing to remember about trust is that it is something you control.

When we are struggling with trust issues relative to a particular person, do we ever ask ourselves why? Is it because they have done something dishonest or is it because they have not proved to us they have a particular level of proficiency? I think that is a critical question that we must answer. If someone has done something dishonest or they have betrayed our trust in some manner, then we need to decide at what level we are going to trust them in that same arena again, and the answer may be "never." That is okay. However, my gut feel is that most trust issues are those of level of knowledge transfer and demonstrated proficiency. For example, I trust Carl Gerhiser to deliver a two-day synchronous flow seminar to our most promising new prospect. Why? The reason is that Carl and I have worked together for nearly 20 years and I have seen him do this workshop many times, so he has demonstrated a repeatable proficiency. That is the basis of the trust.

I trust what Maggie tells me with respect to finding a lost object. Why? I have been on numerous training exercises and actual searches with her and she has demonstrated she knows what she is doing – hence the trust. We are now a much better tracking team. It is not Maggie that has changed, but me. I have absolute confidence in her ability to track and solve problems. I know she feels that. I spend my time on a track not worrying about whether or not we will find what we are looking for, but I spend it trying to read her – is she on the scent or is she trying to relocate it? Does she need me to cast her or does she need a break? Our tracks today are normally very fast and it is all I can do to keep up with her. I attribute much of this to my state of mind and her being able to sense that confidence.

Never in my wildest dreams would I have thought that quoting scripture from the Holy Bible would be applicable in a book using dogs as an example but it has. In John 15:14-15, Christ is talking to his disciples and he refers to them as his friends. Listen to his words, "I no longer call you servants, because a servant does not know his master's business. Instead, I have called you friends, for everything that I learned from my Father I have made known to you." For those of you that are familiar with the story of Jesus you know that his relationship with the disciples evolved from one of teacher/student to one of friend and he states why that is so – "for everything that I learned from my Father I have made known to you." The knowledge base of the disciples reached a point acceptable to Christ that his relationship with them evolved to "friends." It is the same with our friends, associates, and our dogs; we evolve to a certain level of learning and understanding.

So what do you and the ones that you are leading need to do to get to that level of increased relationships? What educational experiences do you need for them to have to bring them to the level where you are comfortable with their competence? Is it a situation where you just need, to recognize that they have had those experiences and you just need to begin to trust more? How much time will that take, and are you willing to invest the effort and wait?

Again, you as the leader control whether or not you want to trust someone. It is a choice. You can either choose to think of someone in a positive manner and view them as a superstar, or you can choose to see them as average or below average. It is your choice. However, there are consequences to that choice. If you choose to see them as something less than a superstar, you do not have to go tell them this – they will feel it just like Maggie felt the stress of the police officers. The business problem is this — information flows through relationships and relationships are

100% based on trust. So if you choose not to trust, you will get crappy relationships and bad information. If you need information to run your enterprise, then your results will be less than you could ultimately achieve.

Over twenty years ago Sherwin-Williams developed a continuous process to manufacture paint and built the plant in Baltimore. To my knowledge, this had never been done before as the classical way of making paint was a batch process. In the new plant, we even tinted the paint continuously; we would inject the colorant into the pipe, send it through an inline mixer, and a spectrophotometer would meter and adjust the color. It was really a hush-hush project as we certainly did not want those nasty competitors learning about this. It was so secret that our own people did not know about it and when they found out many did not believe it. When people came into the plant and saw it operate, they still did not "see it" as they did not "believe it." The project ended up being a failure because too many top dogs at Sherwin-Williams did not believe that paint could be made that way, so they took that plant and converted it back to a traditional batch process.

Several years ago Linda got me a poster for my office that said something to the effect; "you see what you believe, you do not believe what you see." It is so true. If you are struggling with either an employee or your dog, try believing that they are the best darn employee or dog on the planet. If you are successful, you will begin to see that your behavior will be different and thus their behavior will change. It starts with you --- your behavior.

I have had several dear friends review this book before I sent it to the publisher. One friend asked, "On this trust thing – what if I did not get to select my employees? How do I trust them?" What a great question, but the answer is very tough. This is a book on self-reflection as a leader – it is not about them, it is about you. What can you do to make a difference in the trust level? Can you improve their performance by your attitude? I think you can.

Chapter Eight

Rules and Obedience and How They Affect Creativity

The drugs were hidden atop the conference room table. Maggie circled and had her nose all over the table. Many police drug detection dogs may have just jumped up on the table. Janet laughed, "Maggie is too polite and too obedient." There is a fine line of stress between obedience to rules and creativity. You do not want a working dog to get hung up on being obedient at the expense of knocking down their drive to do the job. Rules and obedience have an upside and a down side – the down side is it can crush initiative.

Several months ago we were practicing search and rescue, and Maggie had lost the scent and was working to find it again. I tried to help. Janet instructed, "Maggie is the type of dog that likes to figure stuff out for herself. Let her run with it and she will let you know if she needs assistance." The lesson was to not over manage. Now when Maggie stops and perhaps backtracks some, I will back up and let her work the area until she has it figured out and then we go off again. Part of this is that I know for certain that she knows what she is doing and I can block any negative thoughts from my head on my need to over control.

The more rules we impose the less creativity we have. There may be a temptation to jump to a judgment and say that is bad. Well, not necessarily. I think a lot depends on what type of organization you are in. One of the better business books I have read over the years is *The Discipline of Market Leaders* by Fred Wiersema. In that book, Fred outlines three types of companies; operational excellence, product, and customer intimate. Those three companies approach the market differently and as a consequence, would have different cultures, would hire differently, and would require different levels of compliance to rules.

An Operational Excellence Company wins in the marketplace by being the low cost producer because they are so efficient and normally they deliver commodities. An oil refinery would be a good example and Wal-Mart would be another. A Product Company wins because they come up with breakthrough products – Intel and Apple Computer would be good examples. A Customer Intimate Company focuses totally on the customer and will adapt their standard offerings to meet customer needs.

The DuPont plant I worked for made medical x-ray film. I worked in the coating area where we applied the photo sensitive emulsion to a polyester base. We had very tight specifications on the emulsion and the numerous operating conditions of our coaters and dryers. There was not much wiggle room for non-compliance. To add to the seriousness of this, was the fact that our product was used in the very critical area of disease diagnostics – what we did had to be right as people's lives may depend on it. If we had a better idea on an improved operating condition, we had to go through a long drawn-out testing procedure. That just made sense for that type of operation. We needed excellent quality and the best way to do that was for everyone to do it the same, best way. We had plenty of rules and procedures and non-compliance was not an option.

If there is very little unknown and the processes are relatively repetitive then there is not a whole lot of need for creativity. In such an environment, rules, measures, and procedures in the appropriate quantity to maintain this consistence are good. However, the more and more you are dependent on free thinking and innovation, these rules can actually get in the way.

Let me digress back to some dog training issues and then see if we can draw some human parallels. There is a fad now with some dog trainers and suppliers of military and police dogs, that they do not want any obedience training until they learn their job – sniffing out drugs, bombs, being a patrol dog, etc. The idea is that they want the dog totally focused on the job and not worried about obedience rules. I think there is something to be learned. In search and rescue, when Maggie is on a track she leads and will pull on the leash. In walking down the street I may not want her to pull on her leash. How is she to know whether or not it is appropriate to pull on the leash? As sort of an experiment, I have been on a little "anti-obedience" campaign with Maggie. I cut her some slack when walking on a leash and I no longer use a prong collar for our walks. If it gets too out of hand, I simply stop and say "with me" and she gets the point and it is no big deal. If I give her the command for a competitive heel – fus, then that is something different to her, she will pop her head around and heel while looking at my face. What I have learned is that she seems to be even better on a track and seems to be even more focused than before. It is hard to explain and I would hate to measure it.

Some rules and regulations are tradition under the guise of training. The military, and especially the service academies, have a ton of those, from the way you wear your uniform and make your "rack" (bed) to how you relate to particular individuals. Again, these rules have a specific purpose and you are certainly not looking for any creativity out of a plebe or a recruit. The rules change and get less restrictive the more longevity and rank one gets. For example, a senior at the Naval Academy has a lot more freedom and leeway than a plebe. The same thing applies to our dogs. The older they get and the stronger the relationship and trust, then the less rules we impose on them. The upper classmen are trusted more because they are more knowledgeable with regard to the environment.

As you get into less structured organizations and you want to capitalize more on human potential, then the amount of control you exert over someone directly relates to the level of trust you have in that person.

Control freaks might work out really well in a highly structured, non-innovative environment; however most businesses are not like that. The control freaks, although they look like they are working like the dickens, are actually hindering creativity and productivity – especially their own.

There is an odd relationship between rules, control, discipline, and creativity. Some of the best jazz musicians were first very good at classical music and were disciplined to practice scales and other exercises for hours a day to master their instrument. The same is true for some of the best athletes; Jerry Rice, Nolan Ryan and Walter Payton were all known for their off season work out regimens. These professionals mastered the basics so they no longer had to consider them, leaving more capacity for creative, productive work.

What do your folks need to master in order to have more capacity for productive work? What rules and regulations do you have in place? How do the rules and regulations foster and enable better performance?

It is a more complex question than it appears. It has been my experience that the need for rules and control decreases with the level of trust, and the level of trust for a particular person and situation changes over time as the person's skills and experience evolve. Carl has been with Chesapeake Consulting for nearly two decades. If Carl redoes one of our courses for a particular client or does something off the beaten path, I simply do not worry about it. The only reason I even want to know about it is for my own education and perhaps something we can convey to other consultants. We just hired a new consultant that has never given our course before. I want them staying to a standard course until they are much more comfortable with the technology and the job of working as a consultant at Chesapeake. I need to know a certain level of knowledge transfer has occurred before my trust level goes up.

We do not have a lot of rules and procedures at Chesapeake Consulting because we focus more on the individual consultant verses our process. In consulting, results come from an interaction between the client, the individual consultant and the processes the firm employees. Many organizations (including Dr. Goldratt), relied mostly on their process – all of the major consulting firms rely heavily on their processes and some even sell their processes to clients. Their thought is they can go out and get any MBA grad, teach them the process, and off they go.

Chesapeake Consulting takes the opposite approach. Yes, we like our processes too, however we feel the individual consultant and their life experiences is much more important and we can be more effective when we walk into chaotic environments. Too many rules would mess us up. Additional barriers would also cause trust level to go down among our consultants. Many times dogs will bark when behind a fence. Take the fence down, the trust level goes up and the barking stops.

In summary, a lot depends on how many rules and procedures you have or do not have. Probably the best advice is to set up a schedule to constantly analyze. In our consulting practice using TOC, we have learned that physical constraints are caused by policy constraints (rules) which are caused by mindsets (beliefs). Many times a rule, policy, or procedure that is put in for a specific cause is so effective that it invalidates the rule thus it can be eliminated, however the erroneous mindset may still be in place. It is a moving target and you as the leader need to be in an evaluation mode.

Chapter Nine

Reward, Punishment, and Stress

Maggie was a young dog and we were walking on the sidewalk near our house. A car slowly drove by and Maggie lunged for the car as if she wanted to chase it. I immediately yelled "NO" and yanked her leash so hard it knocked her down. I then faced her, grabbed her by both sides of her mouth, looked her directly in her eyes, and shook her as I lambasted her behavior. I wanted her to have an awful experience associated with lunging at that car. She cowered down, ears back, and tail between her legs. I ignored her. What Maggie just experienced was a hard correction. She never lunged at another car nor has she even hinted she has any desire to chase one. Chasing a car would endanger her life and thus warranted a hard correction.

Unwarranted aggression with humans or other dogs are other reasons for a hard correction which is both a verbal and a physical correction. Never, ever hit a dog. Grabbing the nap of the neck (like their mother did) or grabbing the sides of their neck or mouth and shaking is sufficient. You run no risk of hurting the dog and it gets the point across that whatever they did will not be tolerated. You will also want to give stern eye contact that you are angry. Many times a stare from the alpha wolf will get a subordinate in line. After you give a hard correction, put your dog in a down and ignore him for a few minutes. Then make up.

When you establish a good relationship with your dog, then normally a "nope" will be sufficient to get your point across.

In training, never correct the dog unless you are absolutely certain the dog understands what you want them to do and they just decided to tell you to take a long walk off a short pier. Training needs to be "fair, firm, and fun." Your dog should look forward to being with you. And again, quick leash corrections and short verbal corrections are normally all that is needed.

I had been at Sherwin-Williams several months and we were making progress, but we were also making changes that were uncomfortable to those that had been there for a long time. Most of my staff were people who had been at the site for years, only my controller and the HR director were new. We were in our weekly staff meeting going over some plans and my maintenance superintendent, Walt said, "Why should we do anything that you say? You won't be here that long anyway. None of our plant managers make it very long. They either quit or get fired." Walt was correct. However, what just happened was a coup attempt; one of my dogs had bit me in front of the rest of the pack. It was a bold move on Walt's part.

I responded, "Walt, you are correct. However the reason you should do what I say is that if you don't you will not be around here to see me leave." And he wasn't. He basically called my bluff and never got in alignment with what we were trying to get accomplished.

What is the purpose of punishment or correction at work? In dogs, it is pretty straightforward. We want to help mold the dog to where they are a good citizen and can adequately co-exist with their humans. However dogs get "fired" also. Many dogs wash out of search and rescue, seeing eye dogs, and police and military duty. It is a simple matter that they are not skilled, driven, or motivated for that type of work and that is not a problem. The worst case scenario is that they become a house pet and live a "dogs life" which in most houses is a pretty neat existence. One of my daughter's friends once said, "If there is such a thing as reincarnation, I want to come back as a Covington family pet."

I have never found it real useful to do a lot of "punishing" in the work environment. There are the cut and dried cases of poor attendance, stealing, substance abuse, and serious insubordination, but those are rare. Normally what works at work is a well worded question. Your folks will react to the questions you ask. If you are skilled at asking questions, then pretty soon the subordinate will end up discovering for themselves the error of their ways and will take corrective action. When asking questions, ask questions that begin with "what." "What results do you expect from this program? What do you think about that? What are you doing?" What questions cannot be answered with a yes or no and require some dialogue. Many times what is surfaced is a simple misunderstanding.

However sometimes it is not a misunderstanding but a difference in philosophy or a failure to be in alignment with a new direction. It has been my experience that if I keep the new direction in focus for everyone and it becomes clear that I am going to see it through, that some people will elect to leave. The culture will change and they will be ejected like a virus. Linda once observed, "You never fire anyone, you just drive them crazy and they quit."

Now that we have talked about the punishment side of the equation, let's talk about the reward. Positive motivation is vastly superior to compulsion. Compulsion should only be used in extreme situations such as lunging at a car, direct insubordination, stealing from an employer, etc. Compulsion for dogs is always physical/verbal and at work it is verbal/discipline related.

Dogs trained today using positive techniques outperform dogs trained using the old compulsion yank and tug methods. The first step is to find out what motivates your dog. There are four things that I use to excite and motivate Maggie – a ball, a tug, bits of food, and just some plain excitement. If she sees one of her motivators, she will start offering up behavior to do anything she can to get her reward. If I pull out her ball, she will first jump around and try and take it from me then she will start going into a sit, a down, or anything she figures it is that I want her to do. Once motivated, all I have to do is point out a direction and she will do it as long as she knows what I want.

I personally do not think we use positive motivation enough in leading people

Why is it that we as leaders sometimes revert to compulsion/coercion? Under what situation do you use compulsion with your dog? I find it is when I lose patience or my ego somehow has been bruised. With dogs and people, leaders need to check their ego at the door.

How we can we look for positive re-enforcement more often?

Several of us "working dog" people were sitting around discussing the issue of getting a dog to "out" after a bite. In protection work, the decoy, at the very minimum, has a padded sleeve. Dogs that excel in protection work consider it a great reward "to get a bite," which means they are okayed to run and bite the decoy. However it is important for the dog to let go when you tell them. In a dog's world, anything that they have in their mouth belongs to them – so not only does the dog enjoy biting the sleeve, they also possess the sleeve—it is theirs. Getting them to "out" is a trick. Most people that I have seen use compulsion to get the dog to release, including me. When Maggie is locked on to her tug and will not out when I tell her, I used to take my index finger and give her a little pop on the nose. In bite work one normally lifts the dogs' feet off the ground by their collar and they drop the sleeve. By the way, this is on a flat collar so it does not hurt the dog.

Recently I have not popped Maggie on the nose but have done two things – first I will bribe her with something else to get her to release and then I will let her bite her tug immediately after she releases it to let her know that I am not going to keep it from her. I want her to trust me; I want her to understand that whenever I tell her to do something and she obeys, it works out well for her. I have recently seen her "outs" become much quicker. Part of the solution here is for me to look at the situation from Maggie's point of view. She is in possession of the tug and is having a great time playing with me. If I release the tug and back-peddle, she will immediately chase after me shoving the tug against me and wants me to engage her in the game of tug. She is having fun and she wants the fun to continue. I need to align my actions in such a way to let her know that she is not going to lose by "outing" her tug.

Linda and I were traveling to our best friends' house. Our friends are helping to raise their teenage granddaughter and it has been tough. In our discussion Linda said, "They need to tell her she needs to get her act together or else!" Sounds a tad like compulsion – it is a good thing for the granddaughter that she is not wearing a prong collar with Linda holding the leash.

What would motivate the granddaughter to "behave?" First of all, someone would have to look at the entire situation from the granddaughter's point of view and begin to craft a solution from there. What would motivate her?

People and dogs act different under stress. One of the assessments we give people is the DISC assessment for behavior traits. One of the outputs from the analysis is how someone may act under stress. The wise leader observes undesirable behavior and then must ask themselves, is this a stress issue for the employee or dog? If it is, then what can the leader do to relieve the stress? I guess the first order of business is to determine whether or not you are the one causing the stress. If you are, and the stress you are causing is unintentional, then you must adapt your behavior to help solve the problem. Take into consideration, there are times when it is appropriate to cause stress – just be sure and know the difference.

I earlier related a story about Maggie being on a track looking for Lucinda and that she was stressed. Now, I can read her well enough to know when she is stressed and can take corrective action. If your dog is stressed, simply put them on a down and talk nice to them, and if that doesn't do it, rub their tummy with your open hand. That is probably not going to work with your employees. You will need to figure out something else.

When Maggie is on a track and I see that she is getting stressed, we take a short "stress break" and when we are done I re-introduce the scent item and off we go again. So far that has worked like a charm.

With both dogs and people, try and avoid negative stress if possible.

In summary, punishment/correction/restrictions are part of the learning and development process, but need not be the primary motivator. The good leader looks for more rewards for a job well done. Many times that may just be a "thank you." One of Maggie's biggest rewards is to be engaged in meaningful work with me. She knows when she is going to S&R training or getting ready to go on an actual search. She is excited and is almost uncontrollable with anticipation. That may be the same with humans. My biggest reward is working with some of our folks and a client to solve some problem.

Chapter Ten

Bias in Dogs and People; It's a Good and Bad Thing

One of my favorite dogs of all time was my little buddy Henry. Henry was a Cairn Terrier and quite a character. You can read many of Henrys' escapades in my book *Let's Don't Pave the Cow Paths.*

One day when visiting my in-laws in Alabama, Henry and I went out back for a stroll. At the time my, father-in-law had some cows in the pasture and an electric fence to keep them contained. I stepped over the fence and Henry, his tail straight out from his body, trotted under the fence. When it came time to come in, I stepped back over the fence and Henry was taking his time as he was checking out one of the cows. I gave him a quick call and here he came -- tail riding high in the air and he was full of energy. However, when he ran under the fence, this time his tail struck the electric wire. He let out a yelp, whirled around and the only thing he saw was a cow. He was furious at that cow! He growled and barked and did everything else in his arsenal to let that cow know how displeased he was that the cow bit his tail. Cows were now bad and every time he saw one from that point on, Henry expressed his displeasure. There was no convincing him otherwise. Cows are just bad news.

Many times in search and rescue (S&R) training we use those little surveyor flags to mark where to begin a track and where the person laying the track may have made a turn. Especially in the early stages of training there are normally treats on the track so the dog learns that good things come from keeping their nose to the ground tracking their prey. You have to be careful because pretty soon the dogs learn that those flags probably mean there is food on the trail nearby. Maggie and I were visiting in Alabama and I was taking her for a walk on the University of Alabama campus. We were in a large field with no one around so I had her off leash. However, they were laying the place out for construction and there must have been a 100 of those little flags stuck all over the ground. Maggie went nuts! Obviously she had died and gone to doggie heaven as this was going to be a hotdog treat paradise. She eagerly went from flag to flag and soon her disappointment was obvious. She began the walk with a strong bias that there was food associated with each one of those flags, however her experience proved otherwise. Her bias was changed only through actual experience.

It was in the early 1970's and myself and several other white males were leaving a physics lab at night. We were walking down University Avenue and a young black woman was driving an oncoming car. She saw us and leaned over and locked the door on the passenger side of the car. She had pre-judged us to be a potential threat based on our age, color, and gender. As she drove by, we made eye contact and I smiled. She looked as if to say, "I'm sorry." I thought, "It's okay – I understand. I do the same thing."

Bias is not totally a bad thing and many times it serves to protect us. Would you want your wife or daughter walking alone in a scary neighborhood at night? Your bias tells you that would not be a good idea. That bias is learned and somewhere along the line those types of biases protect us from harm and help us along life's way. However, these biases can also hinder us in improvement in both people and dogs.

Lee was a rescued dog from North Carolina that had been abused by males and developed a bias against males. Lee was supposed to be a hunting dog. However, he did not do well in the field and his male owner abused him because he could not hunt well. Fortunately, he was rescued because the owner wanted to take him out and shoot him. Whenever a man approached Lee, he would cower down and back away. I was determined to make friends with Lee. As I approached, I tossed a piece of hotdog his way. Eventually I worked with him so he would come and take the hotdog out of my hand – but would grab the hotdog and make a hasty retreat. I would only see Lee on Saturdays as his owner would bring him to "doggie school." After about eight months of knowing me, Lee now bolts toward me and wants to play when he sees me coming. He is also okay with other men. The bias had to be broken with a positive experience.

Biases are nothing more than assumptions. If you make the general assumption that people and dogs are basically good then most negative biases/assumptions are erroneous. Actually, that is some pretty good news. If somehow you can expose the bias to be erroneous, then you can make forward progress with the relationship and whatever mission you are trying to achieve.

In people and in dogs, the only way to overcome bias is with experience. Just talking to them or trying to convince them with data is not going to work. They either need to have hands-on experience or a really good parable that gets them to have an experiential feeling.

In organizations physical constraints to performance are normally caused by policies, which are based on our belief systems, our assumptions about life, and our biases. In order to change the policy that causes the blockage to improvement, one must address the bias through taking those involved through an experience.

I am an approved evaluator for the American Kennel Club's Canine Good Citizenship test. One of the exercises in the test is how a dog does with another approaching dog. Let's say the dog has a tendency to lunge at an approaching dog. This dog has some sort of bias – it either thinks the other dog is going to hurt it or they are convinced the other dog is going to hurt their owner. The dog needs to have some good experiences that negate that bias. You would begin with an experience such as   walking behind another dog 20 feet or so and gradually decrease the gap until you are walking side by side with the other dog. Do that several times and pretty soon the dog has an experience that convinces them that their previous bias was erroneous.

I had just finished an assignment with a client and was at the Milwaukee airport waiting to catch my flight. I found a nice secluded part of the gate area, plopped down, and began to read, relax, and wait for my flight. A black man with a large gold chain around his neck, baggie pants, baseball hat with flat brim on his head sideways, and was talking jive talk on his cell phone loud enough for me to hear sat down across from me. I sensed myself getting irritated. Soon a nice looking lady sits beside him. How could a nice, clean cut looking lady be with that clown? It was about seven PM and this guy was constantly on the phone. I finally eavesdropped and listened to his conversation – he was a small business owner, a contractor, and he was calling employees, suppliers, and getting things organized for the next day – he was working. Of all the people on the plane, I had more in common with him than anyone. We boarded the plan and he and his wife were in first class with me. By the way, the reason I was in first class is I have so many flying points I could almost claim the entire plane as mine. Not only was I in first class, but the seat next to me was empty. Right before the door closed a young black man dressed ten times worse than the older guy boards the plane and his seat is next to me. He looks at me with the same sort of "ut-oh" that I was looking at him. My bias was that this young man had somehow missed the prison bus and Lord knows what he was thinking. Neither of us looked pleased based upon our biases. I made the first conversation before take-off and we talked each other's ears off the entire flight. He was a delightful young man and a college student at the University of Maryland. In about an hour time, frame reality hit me over the head twice because of my bias.

Dogs seem to get over their biases easier than people. If you show a dog a better way to do something – even if they have been doing it the same way all of their life – a dog will change.

Sometimes people take a little longer and, like dogs, they will need to have an actual experience that will break the bias. Sometimes we need a whack over the head at an airport.

In our business, we constantly deal with the bias that people have. There is an old saying that the definition of insanity is to keep doing the same thing over and over again and expect different results. We do those things over and over again because of our belief systems. In order to do it differently, we must be able to change our mindsets – our biases. We use a variety of games, simulations, lectures, and stories to take our client through an experience that will chip away at those productivity hindering biases. CCI telling the client that their bias is incorrect is not going to work; they must discover it for themselves. That is the only way in the long run that a positive change will be sustained.

Chapter Eleven

Motivating Dogs and People

Customers buy for their reasons – not yours. Employees do things for their reasons – not yours. Dogs do things for their reasons – not yours. Darn – how about them apples? Life is just not fair when we are not the number one consideration.

You do not have to be around a bunch of dog handlers long when you begin to hear about "food drive" or "play drive" or "hunt drive" and every other type of drive you can think of.

In training dogs, you hear people talk about reward based and compulsion-based methods. In reward-based training, the dog obeys a command in anticipation of something good. In compulsion, it obeys a command to avoid a negative consequence. In talking with people in the dog community, there is no doubt that reward-based is much more effective than compulsion. Dogs in competitive sports such as agility and Schutzhund are much sharper than they were years ago when compulsion was the primary way to train dogs — the yank and jerk method, referring to the yank and jerk on the leash.

The idea behind reward based training is that the dog is rewarded for a given behavior. The reward needs to be administered immediately. I have read where one has 1.5 seconds between the time a dog executes a particular behavior and when you must reward. That is why some use "clicker training" or a bridge word to recognize the good behavior with the promise that your reward is imminent and on its way.

I use four rewards with Maggie – food, play, petting, and verbal praise. One thought for those that use food as a reward is to allocate a certain percentage of your dogs' daily calories in treats, so not only is your dog well trained it also does not look like a Basset balloon . In the initial phases of training I use food because dogs can be lured with food. A good rule to remember is whatever direction the nose goes, the tail goes in the opposite direction. If you want the dog to sit, hold the treat above his nose headed back towards his skull and his butt will plop on the ground. As soon as their tail feathers touch the grass, use your bridge word and give the reward.

I enjoy using play for a reward once the dog knows what it is supposed to do. I like playing tug as it is interactive between you and the dog. If done right, it can also be good exercise especially if you have a large dog.

With dogs there is a phrase – "nothing in life is free." That means the dog must do something cool for anything it gets. Maggie must sit and stay before I put her food dish down.

In determining the reward for your dog, you will need to learn what motivates the dog. I have had people tell me that their dog is not motivated by food. My smart aleck answer to that obstacle is "you are feeding your dog too much."

As my friend Jerry Bradshaw says, "Dogs are opportunistic predators and they are great manipulators of their environment." The dog does not do something in order to please you; it does something because it expects something in return.

Let's talk about human motivators for a minute. I think listing Maslow's Hierarchy of needs is a good place to start. Those needs are:

1. Biological and Psychological (food, water, rest, warmth, etc)
2. Safety Needs

3. Belongingness and Loving (Intimate relations, friends)
4. Esteem Needs (feeling of accomplishment)
5. Self-Actualization (achieving one's full potential, creativity)

There are six work motivators we test for:

1. Traditional – folks that score high here seek a system for living such as religion.
2. Social – folks that have a high regard for people. These people would donate a lot to charity and are kind, sympathetic.
3. Individualistic—primary interest may be power and influence.
4. Theoretical – someone with this as a motivator may seek the "truth" and they love to learn new stuff. Some may appear to be an intellectual.
5. Utilitarian—someone who may be motivated by money and wants a return on their time.
6. Aesthetic—indicates a high interest in art and form and harmony in life.

So if you are trying to motivate someone with money who is not high utilitarian, it may be the same as trying to motivate a dog with food that has no food drive. The first step in motivation is to understand what a particular individual or group of individuals considers important.

The lists of needs and motivators above gives us a clue as to how to motivate people.

Ralph Stokes is great friend of mine and one of the first African-American football players at the University of Alabama. A reporter once asked him if Coach Paul "Bear" Bryant treated everyone equal. Ralph answered, "No—he treated everyone fairly. Some people needed a swift kick in the pants and others needed an arm around their shoulder. Coach Bryant understood who needed what."

Sometimes us leaders talk about motivation of dogs and people as if we controlled everything. It was an initial shock to me that I do not control everything (much to the delight of my wife). Jerry Bradshaw was saying that if you are training a competition dog and it does not have any food drive, prey drive, etc – get another dog. The same goes for our organizations. If a person gets up every morning and they want to look at art and save the world and they cannot connect the dots between your machine shop and what motivates them, then you both may want to consider different employment for that person.

It has been my experience that we do not put a lot of effort into motivating people; many times we say they should be self-motivated. I know I feel that way many times and I am not convinced that is wrong. There are many folks that are motivated by their team or company being successful. The good leader needs to clearly state the objectives and goals of the organization and provide a good culture in which to work, and that is probably good enough for most people.

A good friend of mine has a granddaughter that is giving her parents fits. The young lady, Jenny, is about 15 and her parents are divorced. She lives with her mom, her step dad and two other siblings that are the children of her mom and step dad. The step dad is in the Navy and they relocate often. Jenny seems to be dissatisfied with everything, which is probably not uncommon for a teenager. Her latest behavior problem involved not going to school, and when she was in school, misbehaving to the point where she was sent to the office. The vice principle finally said – "we are not going to discipline you anymore; we are just going to suspend you." Well – that is exactly what Jenny wants. I asked my friend what motivated Jenny. He thought for a while and said that she pitched an absolute fit when they took her smart phone and texting privileges away from her. She pitched such a fit, they gave them back to her. My advice to my friends was that Jenny's motivator is that smart phone. After she understands that pitching a fit is not going to work and the only path to the smart phone is through going to school and behaving, I bet performance will pick up.

Let's take a look at a specific dog example. If I give Maggie a hard correction and fuss at her, she will cower down, ears back and look pretty pitiful – she is a very handler sensitive dog. If you give a very dominant dog the same correction that dog might say to itself, "Hey, want to get tough? Bring it on!!" Shawn, a friend who heads the K9 unit of a major police force uses a prong collar for his dog's bite work. Normally a flat collar is used as you would not want to have the dog give itself a correction – you want them to be aggressive in bite work. However Shawn's dog, Stewie, actually gets more riled up. Stewie's main motivator is being able to get to bite the decoy and he will do just about anything for that privilege. In some respects, Jenny may be the same way. Giving her a hard correction by suspending her just makes her dig her heels in more. However if that smart phone were the issue, I bet the attitude would eventually change.

Do we focus on motivation with problem employees more? I don't know but my gut feel tells me yes.

What motivates me is I want to be able to use my skill and talent to help make a difference with clients unencumbered by hogwash. We want to hire consultants that want the same thing. In any organization there needs to be something unique or inherent in that group that is exciting to the individual members. A story told many times is about one of the janitors at NASA when asked what his job was. He answered, "I am helping to put a man on the moon." There are individual motivators, but the main motivator needs to be that of the team or work unit.

Chapter Twelve

Training Dogs and People and How It Impacts Trust

My friend and first trainer, Charlie, invited Maggie and me to join him and his pup, Barkly, for some tracking work. The first step is to lay a track. We did this by stomping down the grass in a small circular area and filling it with some hotdog goodies. Then we proceeded out of the circle scuffing as we walked (in order to have a nice vegetation rupture smell) and placed a hotdog bit inside our footsteps on a frequent basis. At the end of the short track, we made another stomped down circle filled with hotdog bits and perhaps a toy. We then would bring a dog up to the circle and they would keep their nose to the ground as they smelled their way along the hotdog laden path. The idea is for the dog to soon associate the smell of the track with the smell of a reward. As the dog progresses, the distance is increased and the frequency of the hotdogs is decreased. Soon turns are introduced and then different types of surfaces including hard surfaces such as asphalt and concrete. Then scent discrimination is added to the mix and the tracks are purposely contaminated to make sure the dog stays on the scent they are supposed to be looking for. At the end of each track, there is a big reward and payoff for the dog in food or a play session with a toy or both.

Although the dogs' natural instincts are employed, there is a specific way to hunt for someone or something that is lost. Even if Maggie could read, I do not think she would learn tracking by reading it in a book because it is different than the way she would naturally do it. Having the discipline to keep her nose on the ground and "footstep" track rather than "air scent" makes her a better search dog. She can air scent when she is confident that she can go directly to the target and all tracks end with her air scenting. The key thing here is that Maggie learned through experiencing the track.

In a recent tracking seminar, the instructor was talking about training search dogs. He said they start with a dog that has no aggression, has good prey drive, a drive to search, and the motivation to work. They start with footstep tracking (Schutzhund or IPO tracking). The training takes 6-12 months and they start the pups at 8 weeks. He said there are three steps to the training; learning phase, construction phase, and the required phase.

I am on several advisory boards with the college of engineering at the University of Alabama. More and more you hear educators talk about "experiential learning." What types of experiences do you want the student to have in order to master a particular topic. One of the best college courses I took was what chemical engineers called "summer lab." Summer lab was like a boot camp for chemical engineering students. We were divided up into teams of 3-5 people and given five experiments that we had to successfully complete by the end of the summer. We had keys to the building, so if we needed to be there 24 hours per day then we could. We all moaned and groaned and only appreciated the impact the course after we had completed it. There was industrial-sized equipment in the lab and it was like working in a real chemical plant. We had to work together as a team and deal with the fact that some contribute more than others. It was a great learning "experience." The key here is that the students experienced something that solidified their learning. Industry values leaning experiences to the point where many employers of engineers insist that a student has had a co-op learning experience. There is a great book on sale by David Sandler, *You Can't Teach A Kid To Ride A Bike At A Seminar*. The kid must actually go out and fall off the bike occasionally.

One of the most important things you do as a leader is train and educate your people on what you want done and perhaps teaching them how to do it, especially if they do not have any experience. The education and knowledge transfer goes a lot deeper than just a level of learning — it goes to a level of trust and we now know that is central to relationships. I hope we are beginning to see and understand that all of this is interconnected... education increases trust, trust improves relationships, information flows through relationships, and information flow forms your organization.

Here is a quote from *Dogs & Devotion*, by the Monks of New Skete, page 53; "There is a reciprocal flow of information in the training process that not only teaches the dog, but teaches us as well, if we're attentive to the moment. Dogs continuously reflect back to us all that we communicate to them either their understanding or lack thereof."

Let's talk some about some of the thoughts on training and educating dogs and see what transfers. Step one is to set up a method of communication with your dog. You need to be able to communicate to the dog whether they have done "good" or not.

Using food as a reward and lure is excellent in the "learning" phase of training. Many of the behaviors you want to train a dog to do are natural to the dog (sit, down, come), so you can take advantage of that. When the dog is starting to sit, say "sit." When it completes the sit use your clicker or bridge word that lets the dog know that a reward is imminent. In the initial learning phase you would want the food visible to entice the dog. Once the dog understands, then hide the food and as soon as you use your bridge word pull out the treat. This begins to build trust – the dog trusts you to give them a reward when you say the bridge word. Trust is the key element in relationships; and remember, this is all about building relationships with your dog.

Once you know that the dog understands that "sit" means sit, then you can begin to introduce corrections in the form of guiding corrections. For example, you say sit, and the dog does not sit, pull up on the leash to guide them into a sit. We are going to pause here for a second and talk about correction. There are all sorts of debates in the dog community with respect to using corrections, and some people are adamant that none should ever be used. I personally think that is unrealistic; however words of caution must apply. Whenever we move towards a compulsion model, we open ourselves up to being less tolerant so it is a slippery slope of action. One of the best examples I have read on the topic was from Michael Ellis, who is a noted dog trainer out of California. He did an experiment with two dogs and did not give them any type of correction their entire life until they were close to two years old. When he gave a correction (applied stress) both dogs reacted poorly; one dog "came up the leash" on him (dog people talk for tried to bite him) and the other dog totally shut down and lost confidence. Ellis attributed this to the fact that the dogs never learned how to deal with stress. Ellis now intentionally introduces some form of stress to a dog before they are one year old. With a prong collar, he will pull back some and as soon as the dog reacts and takes tension off the leash, he lets the leash go and praises the dog. The dog is learning that it can face some level of stress and all will be okay.

I personally think what we have learned over the last several decades is that all positive stress with the absence of negative stress does not work in the long run, and it is not in the best interest in either the dog or the human that we are trying to train. Part of knowledge transfer is learning how to recover after a failed attempt and suffering the consequences of that failed attempt. The summer lab I referred to is a controversial course and many who are outside of the chemical engineering department do not see its merits and have pushed to have it eliminated. They claim that the same lessons can be taught by a cooperative education experience. No one associated with the chemical engineering department agrees with them. The professors have built an educational experience that has lots of stress over a prolonged period and the students cannot run away from it. They are also evaluated by their peers at the end of the course, which is another wonderful learning experience.

One of the problems engineering professors have with the modern day student is that they are unaccustomed to failure. Many students either transfer or threaten to transfer the first time they do not get an A+ on a test. In years past, the student would simply work harder to do better next time. Quitting was not an option, or at least not the first option. I have also noticed the same problem when administering constructive criticism to folks in that same age bracket – they will just disappear and not communicate with you again. I feel they are just like the two dogs Michael Ellis raised that did not have any correction until later in life – they did not learn to handle stress.

We recently had a young high school student in our neighborhood commit suicide. All of our hearts are aching. She had excellent grades, was an outstanding athlete, and was beautiful. People just shake their head and wonder and mutter "why." I am concerned that we are not educating people today how to deal with a setback. Can you get knocked for a loop and then demonstrate that you can recover? It is complex and I cannot help but think that Michael Ellis has it right for not only dogs, but also for people. Being exposed to stress for the simple purpose of having to recover from it is probably a valuable lesson. Maybe shielding children from all adversity is doing more harm than good. A large portion of self-confidence is knowing that you can get up after you have been knocked down. If you never get knocked down, you lose that opportunity to learn.

I am forever grateful of having experienced a plebe year at the US Naval Academy. If you would have asked me during that year how I felt, it would have been a different answer. One of the many lessons it taught me is that I could be subjected to an enormous amount of physical and mental stress over an extended period of time and all would be well at the end of the journey. That experience added to my confidence of being able to handle less than desirable situations.

There is a "child psychologist" that writes an article on parenting each Thursday in our local newspaper. He is a fellow after my own heart and he maintains that people like himself made some crucial errors on giving advice on raising children. He maintains that the "high self-esteem" kick did not work. He said that many kids that have the high self-esteem perform poorly, as they feel they already know it all and they have no concept of correction and how to handle it. We have lost balance in our educational efforts.

The other day Maggie and I were walking at the local school where there was a lacrosse game. Around the edges of the playing field were orange plastic cones to mark the boundaries. It was late in the day and the game was almost over. One of the mothers was walking around collecting the cones to take in. I said to her, "You should let the kids do that; you shouldn't be picking those up." She looked at me like I had three heads. She replied, "Well I want to get home sometime tonight." There were enough kids on that lacrosse team to have collected the cones in fifteen seconds. I started to tell her that she was teaching a lesson, but I thought it best to keep my mouth shut. It takes more time and effort to teach rather than just do it ourselves sometime. We need to be in the moment and teach for the benefit of the one learning.

When the dog becomes proficient in an exercise then you are into the reinforcement phase. In this phase, you can totally or partially replace food as a reward and move to other rewards such as a fight with a tug, a ball or toy, or a good old fashion praise and petting session. You would still use your bridge word which both releases the dog from the exercise and sets up the reward.

Everything we do with our dogs we are either strengthening or weakening our trust and relationship with them. Stephen Covey used the phrase making deposits or withdrawals from one's emotional bank account. In the long run, we want to make sure we make more deposits than withdrawals.

As time goes by and the dog becomes more and more proficient in their work, then the confidence and trust builds in both the dog and the handler. They can then almost go into some sort of a dance with regard to their relationship in work and it is much more fun and productive for the team.

In learning to track in search and rescue, there was lots of food on the trail and there were flags marking where turns were and there was normally food associated with the turns. As Maggie progressed, there was less and less food. Today there is no food on the trail unless we are trying to reinforce a principle and she is going stronger than ever on the tracks.

It was interesting how we taught the dogs to track over hard surfaces such as asphalt and concrete. Janet said that our dogs needed to learn that scent can come from hard surfaces. To teach them this skill her boyfriend, Shawn, would take off his shoes (in the winter no less) squirt water on the pavement ahead of his footsteps to lay a track. Shawn is a dedicated boyfriend. Once the dogs learned that scent can come from hard surfaces, then they started checking for it and a hard surface was just like grass with respect to following a track.

At Chesapeake Consulting, the core of our business is employing the concepts of the Theory of Constraints, a management philosophy developed by the late Dr. Eli Goldratt. When we engage a client, we have several phases we go through:

1. An assessment phase
2. An education phase
3. Design and planning
4. Execution

We are essentially training our client how to perform a trick, the trick being to improve their performance.

In the assessment phase, we get a feel for what needs to happen and what knowledge we need to transfer to the client. In phase two, we put the client through "experiences" intended to transfer that knowledge. In phase three, we work with the client to design how the principles will be used in their particular environment, and in phase four we go do it. Learning occurs in each phase and hopefully by the end it is routine for the client and we can go off and work with another client.

Excellent leaders are also good teachers. Knowledge transfer increases levels of trust, which in turn improves relationships, which in turn improves communications, and thus we have a great cycle of improvement and robust leadership. How about that?

In summary, the education of the people working for you is one of the smartest things you can do to improve relationships and the company culture. For the most part, education needs to be experienced based.

Chapter Thirteen

Communications and Listening with Dogs and Humans; Are We Listening?

"Yes!" --- feed a hotdog; "Yes!"--- feed a hotdog; "Yes!"---feed a hotdog. What I am doing is establishing a communications system with my dog by letting her know that the word "Yes" is the bridge between her doing something good and her getting a reward. Again, whenever a dog does something you want and you wish to reward them, you have 1.5 seconds to act. The dog learns that when they hear the bridge word that a reward is immanent.

On the other hand, a loud "NO!" means there may be a leash correction or worse to follow. It clearly means to stop doing that immediately. A simple "nope," means the same thing but not as severe. A long drawn out goooood means keep doing what you are doing. You and your dog will end up developing a special language to where you can communicate with one another. It works both ways. When Maggie begins pacing the floor, goes by me, and hits my legs, she is telling me she wants to go outside. When she drops a toy in my lap, she wants to play. A paw on my knee is an indication that she wants some attention, and perhaps a scratch behind her ears is in order. On a track when she turns around and looks at me with her tail not wagging and her mouth open, it means she has lost the track and wants some help in finding it. As mentioned before, we do a lot of communications with our eyes.

In order to develop a communication system with your dog, you must listen because the dog is giving you continuous feedback as to whether or not you are effective. I hope my wife does not read this, otherwise I am going to catch some grief over this as she has been telling me this for decades. Not long ago she said, "You pay more attention to the dog than you do me." I replied, "If you were to meet me at the door each evening wagging your tail and trying to lick me all over, I would pay more attention to you." I learned that sometimes husbands just need to keep their mouths shut. My dog has taught me that.

How important is communication? Well, no relationship can grow when communication is messed up. Information and communications flow through the relationship, so they are critical for each other.

With your dog, you need to listen more with your eyes by observing body language and correlating it to specific situations. I know when her head is down and she is sleaking around that Maggie is distressed and probably a thunderstorm is on the way. If Maggie is your search dog – do not get lost in a thunderstorm or you will be there for a while. A slow steady tail wag with her nose down on a track means she is on the scent and I simply need to keep up with her. Her head level but lowered below her torso means a killer squirrel may be lurking up ahead and she wants to be ready to pounce. Ears erect, back stiff, head up means she is ready for work/play. It is time for chasing a ball or a game of tug and she wants to know what she has to do to engage.

I have learned a lot about watching the body language of my dog and it gives me enormous insight into how she feels and therefore what I need to do. I am just downright embarrassed that I have not done the same with people I am responsible for in a leadership position. Some situations are obvious. If an employee comes into my office with her head down and is crying her eyes out, that might be an indication that she is distressed. But other than that "frying pan over the head" type of symptom, I am pretty clueless. That is a definite leadership weakness.

Not only is our dog a good lab for practicing our own listening skills, including listening with our eyes, but watch how our dogs listen to us. All dog owners have seen the inquisitive head cock as our dogs are struggling to understand us. Note how your dog watches your face for a clue as to "what's next." Some experts claim that our dogs focus on one side of our face – the side that first gives away our emotions because they know our emotions affect their world.

When I ran manufacturing facilities, I would try and tour the plant twice per day; in the morning and again in the afternoon. After my morning tour, I would have my human resource director tour after me and make sure I had not irritated anyone or been misunderstood on an issue. One of the questions I would ask routinely would be, "How is it going?" This was before I leaned the power of the "what" questions. When someone said, "Okay," I normally knew that it was not okay and it was a cue for me to dig a little deeper. I would always try and make eye contact which meant that sometimes I would need to hang around longer until the person actually looked up and into my eyes. Lack of eye contact may be another indicator that all is not well and that you as the leader may need to be sensitive to that.

If only we leaders could put such effort and a premium on listening.

Summary

This is my fifth book and by far it has been the hardest to write. There is so much knowledge to be gained by exploring the relationship between humans and dogs, and through the process of this effort, I find my head reeling with new knowledge and understanding.

So what have we learned? I am going to try and summarize what I have learned about leadership from my dog.

I learned to put more effort into the selection process:

What are you trying to get accomplished by getting a dog – what is your goal? There are many possibilities:
- You want a companion dog – a loyal pet.
- You are a bleeding heart dog lover and want to give as many rescues their "fur-ever" home.
- You love a certain breed and you just want one to be around.
- You enjoy dog sports and competition.
- You want to detect drugs or explosives.
- You need your sheep or kids herded.
- You want your house protected.
- You enjoy seeing your cat being chased.
- You want a dog for the kids.
- You want a dog to go bird hunting with you.
- You are blind and want a Seeing Eye dog.

Verbalize why you want a dog and then ascertain what types of checks or tests you need to make the selection. Make sure the dog passes all of your tests and checks first and then go with "cute and I like the one with the spot on their nose."

The same certainly goes for people. What is it you need to happen in your organization that is not going to happen unless you make a successful hire? What types of tests, assessments, and background checks do you need to employ to insure that the humans you are evaluating can execute the work you need done. Your selection criteria may include past performance, certifications, motivators, and perhaps personality types. It may also include age and that is all right. I am not going to hire a 60 year old to model a swim suit I am trying to sell to 15 year olds. How much time are you willing to wait until your new hire is to the educational level where you can trust them doing the job? The answers to these questions will be different for everyone, however they are critically important. Probably the most important thing you do as a leader is bringing someone new into your organization.

I co-chair an employment networking group at our church for people who have lost their jobs. The purpose of this ministry is to help teach job seekers learn what they need to do to get employment. Since the other co-chair and I have experience in hiring people, we are able to give the perspective from the other side of the desk. The person hiring of course wants to make a good hire, but beyond all costs they do not want to make a bad hire. A bad hire is awful to an organization and cost many more times the annual salary you are paying the new person.

Lesson learned: develop a valid hiring process that predicts who will be productive and be a valuable employee and then stick to it. If need be, hire Jerry Bradshaw to test your candidates.

I learned that my leadership style will need to adapt depending upon the situation and time:

Objects of your leadership go through stages and so do your relationships, thus your leadership style must adapt to where you are in the relationship. Dogs go through four phases – they are puppies, then adolescent dogs, mature adult dogs, and then aging dogs that are in physical decline. In each of the phases, you are always building trust which enhances the relationship. With puppies, the fun, fair, and fun process rings loud and clear. Your puppy is learning basic social skills and you are always trying to set them up to win. Some of the basics are potty training, do not chew the wall down, be nice to strangers, and overall household manners and living arrangements. The adolescent dog may need a little firmer hand and may test your patience. They are poking around always searching for the leader and want to make sure that the pecking order is correct. The adult/mature dog phase is great – as my friend Wes Jenson says, "Just enjoy your dog during this phase." Both you and the dog are communicating well and are having fun. The older dogs needs your ongoing care and understanding and continued deep love as they near the rainbow bridge.

The same thing goes for your children and for your employees. Many of us have been with Chesapeake Consulting for a long time and those years together have driven those relationships. There is not a lot of "discovery" going on among us as we pretty much know how one another will react in certain situations and we know one another's strengths. That developed over time and experience together.

I learned that leadership really is about relationships and that my level of self-awareness is a critical factor in all of my relationships:

I am currently co-teaching a dog training class with the eventual goal being that each handler and their dog pass the AKC Canine Good Citizenship test. The most prevalent problem I am observing is relationships between dog and handler and the handler not providing the nice calm, confident leadership that the dog cherishes. In their book, *How to Be Your Dog's Best Friend,* the Monks of the New Skete suggest that there is a deep spiritual connection between dogs and human being. They go on to suggest that the relationship can be enhanced by some sort of personal spiritual discipline such as meditation. I do not exactly know how to tell you how to accomplish that, but let's experiment here a tad. The next time you are sitting in your den and your dog is at the other end of the room, try and make eye contact with your dog and begin to have good thoughts. For lack of a better term, perhaps engage in a little prayer for your dog with your eyes open thinking about what a great dog she is and how fortunate you are to be her care-taker – say it also with your eyes as you gaze at her. I bet what you will find is your dog will get up and come to you without a word being said. Just touch your dog gently on her side and just be with her. All is calm --- you are calm and are transferring that calm feeling to your dog.

You are going to go out for a walk or to a training session. Is your mind and heart right? If not, do whatever it takes to get it right, whether that is some sort of self-reflection or meditation or prayer. I know this may sound a tad kinky but I actually believe this stuff because that has worked for me and my relationships with humans. I meditate and pray for each of my employees at least once per week. If I plan to have significant contact with an employee or customer that week, I spend time in prayer, meditation, and discernment over the situation. That spiritual component carries over to the actual meeting and I am convinced that my improved attitude radiates out to the other party and it makes for a much better relationship, leadership, and flow of information.

Also think positive. Again, you see what you believe. Believe your dog is the second coming of Rin-Tin-Tin or Lassie. That is what you will see and the dog will feel that and perform better. Same thing goes for your employees and others that you are called to lead – see them as wonderful talented children of God – your brother or sister. You will see that and they will feel it and act accordingly. Try it and you will learn that this is not so kinky. Remember – I am a knuckle dragging engineer that used to run manufacturing plants not some PhD in psychology.

It is all about your own attitude and focusing on your behavior. I love the quote by Linda Tellington-Jones that the Monks used; "When you sit down to work with a creature, simply focus on what you're doing instead of trying for a connection. Seeking too hard or waiting for some kind of heightened contact will not only block your own experience but will also make your animal nervous and self-conscious."

I leaned that I needed to trust my dog if I wanted better performance:

This is a really hard one for me at times. Intellectually I now get it with Maggie; she has a better nose and sense of smell than me and I need to focus on listening to what she is trying to communicate. If she is trying to tell me something but I do not understand, it does not mean she is confused or messed up. What it probably means is that I am confused and messed up and I need to do a much better job of listening to her and figuring out what she is trying to communicate as it could be really important.

Learning to trust Maggie was a lot easier to learn than learning to trust other humans. Janet Dooley's training helped in that regard – she forced the issue. When I trusted Maggie, we were successful in searches for people and drugs, and when I did not trust Maggie, we were unsuccessful. I am no Albert Einstein, but it does not take many of those situations for me to get the point. Let's try and ease into human-human relations.

I received a good chemical engineering education at the University of Alabama and I feel confident in saying that after being out of school for over 40 years. A wise supervisor once told me about relationships with chemical operators, none of which had a college education; "Listen to what your operators are telling you. They may not use the same language you use or they may jump to conclusions but what they are telling you is correct. Listen and then apply your knowledge and see that it is in alignment to what they are saying." That knowledge served me well. Back in the late 1970's I was one of four shift engineers/leaders for the start-up of a brand new plant. It was a complex process that had never been done before and it had not been run in a pilot plant. It was a stressful situation as the company had invested a lot of capital and the start-up was not going well – except on my shift. Soon it became almost embarrassing that my shifts would run well and others would not run so well. What was the secret to my success – I listened to the operators, they listened to me, and we worked together. It was almost that simple.

There is a problem with trusting people and that is sometimes you will be burned. As a small business owner, I have been burned a lot. I have had employees leave and start their own consulting firms and called our clients and used our materials. I have had customers not pay their bills and I had to eat the loss. However that is just part of the game --- if you trust, you will get burned on occasion. So what? The alternative is to choose not to trust and that is not a good choice. When you trust a lot you will be rewarded more than you can imagine, and that makes it worth the occasional disappointment.

I leaned that I needed to be in the moment:

In this moment with me is my dog, the people I work with, my family, and my God. Am I there or am I out to lunch? Is an argument starting to brew in the moment? If so, is it worth it; is that how I want to spend my time in this passing moment? What do I want to accomplish in the moment that will make me a better leader? Part of utilizing the moment is doing some general and daily planning. The more detailed you are about planning your day the better prepared you are for the unexpected moment where you need to be there both physically and emotionally. That may sound counterintuitive, but it is true.

Over the years I have been a fan of Stephen Covey and have adopted his *Seven Habits of Highly Effective People* as a base for my planning. Covey and others say there are four main parts to your being where you need to focus and have improvement plans; physical, mental, spiritual, and social. Physical is pretty obvious – get a physical, exercise, and eat right. Mental improvement might mean working cross word puzzles, reading, or taking an educational class. Spiritual is your relationship with God or whatever it is that floats your boat in that realm. And Social is engaging in time with your family and friends.

He also said to define your roles in life and map out improvement plans for each role. For example, I have roles as husband, CEO of Chesapeake Consulting, chair of our church council, etc. Each day I have specific items to do in the sharpening my saw arena and the rest of the day is filled with role specific tasks. Having a good annual, weekly, and daily plan helps your awareness of the moment and frees up a boatload of time. The advantage to this is you have time for interruptions where you can be in the moment with someone.

In the Preface, I said I would tie in the concepts of *Enterprise Fitness* to this book. Below is the Enterprise Fitness Leadership Model.

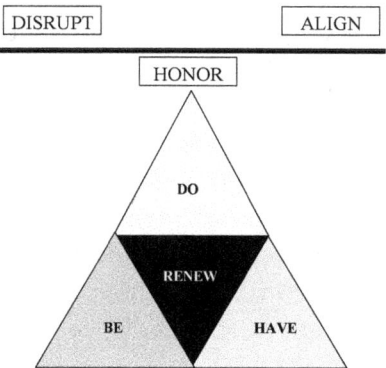

At the top of the pyramid is the DO section. What we should observe leaders doing is Disrupting, Honoring, and Aligning. These are specific actions. For example, when you ask your scheduler, "What impact with this schedule have on due date performance," you just asked a disruptive question. In your mind, you have alignment figured out as better due date performance translates to additional sales. When you are in the moment with your scheduler, you are honoring her. The items below in the pyramid, Have, Be, and Renew are all things that you can work on to become better leaders – things that you can proactively do in the moment. These foundational pieces help you better disrupt, honor, and align.

I learned that I need to learn the language of dogs and of those I am leading:

I was visiting a client that made artificial flowers. During one of our tours of the plant, one worker was highly agitated. He threw several boxes, his arms were flailing away, and he was ranting on and on about something --- in Spanish. I could not understand a word he was saying but it was quite obvious that he was upset. I asked my client, "Do you speak Spanish?" He said that he did not. How do you provide leadership in that environment? How can you empathize and work with your employees if you cannot even understand what they are saying?

Most dog language is non-verbal. When Maggie walks in circles in our den and bumps into my leg the message is, "I have to go pee." When she goes by and stares at her leash she is saying, "I know ya'll are fixing to go somewhere (she is a southern dog) and I most definitely want to be included in your travel plans." When she goes to the back sliding glass door and glances over to me she is saying, "Is there anyway I can hoodwink you into opening this door – I think I saw a cat out there that needs chasing?"

I learned that I needed to be more serious about dominion and its responsibilities:

Everyone has dominion over something and it is an awesome responsibility. You have dominion over your dog. You are the dog's care-taker and protector, the alpha dog. You supply the food, the vet visits, flea and tick medicine, obedience training, socialization, and most of all your time and calm leadership. You are your dog's world.

So how do you do in that area? I bet you do pretty darn good. Most people I have run into do a better job providing for their dogs than they do their families, friends, and employees.

That thought of us doing well with our dogs brings me to some closing comments.

Today's daily devotional from the Upper Room was written by some lady from Arizona who talked about her visits to Hope, Arizona. She said that when you leave the town there is a sign that reads, "You are Beyond Hope." That is a funny sign. This week, my favorite dog trainer, Janet Dooley, had a birthday party for her female English bulldog, Hope. Hope turned eleven years old and rules the roost in a house full of Malinois and German shepherds. I recall sitting across from a client several years ago and asking him, "What gives you hope?" I was taken back when he looked me in the eye and said; "You. You and your company give me hope." Here I am writing a book about leadership and dogs and I am supposed to end with a theme of hope?

Hope for ourselves and those we lead goes back to that dominion thing again. We must recognize our responsibility in helping dogs and others achieve their potential which actually helps fulfill us. If we do our job well, then all concerned have reason for hope – including us.

Let us view our dominion not as a possession or territory or opportunity to wield authority, but as an opportunity to be in the moment, be with our surroundings, and be aware of what we are doing and how it impacts our surroundings.

In my industrial career I managed plants, and it seems I was always sent to the one that was in terrible shape. The person who led the facility before me did not do well at improving the dominion that they were held accountable for. From my perspective, the dominion that I inherited was like getting a dog from the humane society that had been abused and the steps to improvement were similar. Many times when you adopt, the dog needs to be cleaned, fed; basic safety needs met, and needs someone to trust in. That is how I found 100% of the plants I took over. I would first begin with a good safety program, cleanup campaign, and a lot of walking around talking to people to begin to establish relationships and learning the issues. The Sherwin-Williams facility I took over in Baltimore was one that had been purchased from Baltimore Paint and Chemical Company along with other plants in Los Angeles, Chicago, and Philadelphia. All the other plants had been closed and Baltimore was next. The safety record was awful. I learned the people in the red sweat suits were the drug dealers; none of the paint was on time, and if it was, it was poor quality and a variety of other things were messed up. However, within two years the plant was the best performing facility within Sherwin-Williams and won all sorts of accolades. That old mangy mutt won the dog show and the processes for improvement for the plant and the dog were similar. Most of it based on trust and other principles we discussed in this book. I treated the facility like I would my dog and we were successful. You can do the same.

I hope you have a dog in your life, especially if you are a leader. Not only will they teach you improved leadership skills, they will stand by your side on those days when you are quite unlovable to all the others you lead.

www.ingramcontent.com/pod-product-compliance
Lightning Source LLC
Chambersburg PA
CBHW060846050426
42453CB00008B/863